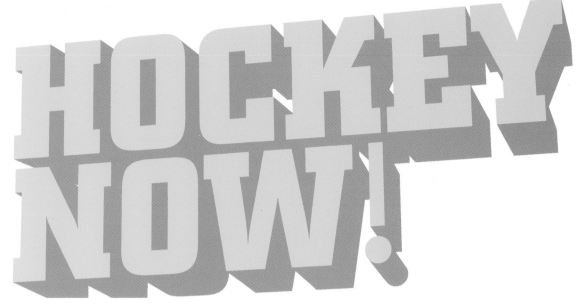

HOCKEY NOW!

TENTH EDITION

THE BIGGEST STARS OF THE NHL

MIKE RYAN

FIREFLY BOOKS

For Christine, my wife and best friend

Published by Firefly Books Ltd. 2019

First printing

Library of Congress Control Number: 2019940487

Library and Archives Canada Cataloguing in Publication
Title: Hockey now! : the biggest stars of the NHL / Mike Ryan.
Names: Ryan, Mike, 1974- author.
Description: Tenth edition. | Includes index.
Identifiers: Canadiana 20190141212 | ISBN 9780228102168 (softcover)
Subjects: LCSH: National Hockey League—Biography. | LCSH: Hockey players—
    Biography. | LCSH: Hockey players—Pictorial works.
Classification: LCC GV848.5.A1 L45 2019 | DDC 796.962092/2—dc23

Published in the United States by
Firefly Books (U.S.) Inc.
P.O. Box 1338, Ellicott Station
Buffalo, New York 14205

Published in Canada by
Firefly Books Ltd.
50 Staples Avenue, Unit 1
Richmond Hill, Ontario L4B 0A7

Cover and interior design: Kimberley Young
Front cover: Curtis Comeau/Icon Sportswire: McDavid
        Jeanine Leech/Icon Sportswire: Crosby
        Joel Auerbach/Icon Sportswire: Burns
        Mark LoMoglio/Icon Sportswire: Vasilevskiy, Matthews
        Patrick Gorski/Icon Sportswire: Kane
Back cover: Jeanine Leech/Icon Sportswire: Rinne
        Mark LoMoglio/Icon Sportswire: Kucherov
        Vincent Ethier/Icon Sportswire: Ovechkin

Printed in Canada

Canada [+] We acknowledge the financial support of the Government of Canada.

TABLE OF CONTENTS

Introduction 5

Atlantic Division 6

Metropolitan Division 44

Central Division 82

Pacific Division 120

Player Index 158

Photo Credits and Acknowledgments 159

INTRODUCTION

Hockey is a numbers game. From traditional statistics to advanced analytics, there are countless ways to quantify a player's worth. For this edition of *Hockey Now!*, I set clear parameters lest I overthink the players to be included and created lineups of three forwards, two defensemen and a goalie for each of the NHL's four divisions. I used my own mysterious calculus of past performance, level of play at the time of choosing (roughly halfway through the 2018–19 season) and future projection to rank the players. It was part science, part gut.

I broke each division's 18 players into a First Team, Second Team and Black Aces — a term thought to be coined by Eddie Shore, a Boston Bruins star in the 1920s and '30s, that was based on poker's "dead man's hand." It refers to the players on a team who aren't on the active roster, the ones waiting and hoping for an opportunity. The Black Aces in here aren't exactly fringe players and castoffs, but the designation is one of hockey's enduring quirks.

Many worthy players have been left out, usually based on a division having a particularly strong corps at one position or because a team was overrepresented. It's a numbers game that plays out at the NHL All-Star Game every season and will always provoke debate.

Some players are certainties for future editions; Roman Josi and John Klingberg were on the rise when I was writing the ninth edition, and now they're firmly established stars. On the flipside is Marc-André Fleury, who was left out of the last edition because it seemed he'd aged out of his glory days. A Pittsburgh Penguins backup then, he had a career renaissance with the expansion Vegas Golden Knights and now is a first-teamer.

The youngest stars in the last edition, Auston Matthews and Patrik Laine, have since experienced the peaks and valleys of professional hockey and seem like grizzled veterans compared with the youngsters in this one, like Elias Pettersson and Rasmus Dahlin. And so the NHL's gears keep turning.

Of course, hockey's hard numbers don't always tell the whole story. Ask the Tampa Bay Lightning, with Vezina Trophy winner Andrei Vasilevskiy and 2018–19 breakout star Nikita Kucherov, who won the scoring title with a Russian-record 128 points, the Ted Lindsay Award and the Hart Trophy. The Lightning strolled to the Presidents' Trophy with an NHL record-tying 62 wins and 128 points, 21 ahead of the next team. They were then summarily swept in the first round by the wild-card Columbus Blue Jackets.

Or ask the Calgary Flames, first in the Western Conference but another first-round casualty. Some solace was found in Flames captain Mark Giordano, who was just the fourth defenseman in NHL history to score 70 or more points at 35 years old, a number that helped him become the fourth player to win the Norris Trophy at age 35 or older.

Four is also the number of goals the San Jose Sharks scored on a five-minute power play in the third period of Game 7 versus the Vegas Golden Knights in the first round of the 2019 playoffs. They erased a three-goal deficit before winning in overtime and eliminating the Golden Knights. Vegas had real championship aspirations after losing in the 2018 Stanley Cup Final to the Washington Capitals and Alex Ovechkin. The Capitals' first Stanley Cup denied the Golden Knights the first ever title for a first-year team. Not since 1968 has a team made the final in its inaugural year, and that team was the St. Louis Blues — the subject of another surprising plot twist in 2018–19.

On January 3, 2019, the Blues were last overall in the NHL, but what a difference five months makes. In Game 7 of the Stanley Cup Final they beat the Boston Bruins. It was their first appearance in the final in 49 years, when St. Louis lost to Boston and Bobby Orr's iconic flying Stanley Cup–winner. Blues captain Alex Pietrangelo lifted the franchise's first Cup after 51 years of defeat, ending the second-longest championship drought in the NHL.

Now at 52 years and counting, it's over to you, Toronto.

ATLANTIC DIVISION

FIRST TEAM

8	**PATRICE BERGERON**	Bruins	Center
10	**NIKITA KUCHEROV**	Lightning	Right Wing
12	**AUSTON MATTHEWS**	Maple Leafs	Center
14	**VICTOR HEDMAN**	Lightning	Defense
16	**SHEA WEBER**	Canadiens	Defense
18	**CAREY PRICE**	Canadiens	Goalie

SECOND TEAM

20	**BRAD MARCHAND**	Bruins	Left Wing
22	**STEVEN STAMKOS**	Lightning	Center
24	**JOHN TAVARES**	Maple Leafs	Center
26	**MORGAN RIELLY**	Maple Leafs	Defense
28	**KEITH YANDLE**	Panthers	Defense
30	**ANDREI VASILEVSKIY**	Lightning	Goalie

BLACK ACES

32	**ALEKSANDER BARKOV**	Panthers	Center
34	**JACK EICHEL**	Sabres	Center
36	**DYLAN LARKIN**	Red Wings	Center
38	**THOMAS CHABOT**	Senators	Defense
40	**RASMUS DAHLIN**	Sabres	Defense
42	**FREDERIK ANDERSEN**	Maple Leafs	Goalie

PATRICE BERGERON

Born in L'Ancienne-Lorette and raised in Charny, a suburb of Quebec City, Patrice Bergeron was a renaissance boy. But there was no doubt about his first love. "Hockey's his passion — it has always been his passion," according to his mother, Sylvie Bergeron-Cleary. "He was, I think, 10 years old when he was taking piano lessons. The instructor thought he was talented. Then one day he came home and said he wasn't going back."

The music teacher had suggested he give up hockey to play piano, so he quit piano. Quitting hockey was never an option, even after he was cut by the Séminaire St-François Blizzard Midget AAA team when he was in 10th grade. The following year Bergeron was named captain, and in his final year of high school he left home to play for the Acadie-Bathurst Titan in the Quebec Major Junior Hockey League.

Bergeron was drafted in the second round, 45th overall, by the Boston Bruins in 2003. He made his NHL debut as an 18-year-old, just three years after he couldn't make the Blizzard, and finished his rookie season with a gold medal at the 2004 World Championship. He then won gold for Canada at the 2005 World Juniors, making him the first player in history to win gold at the junior level after doing it with the senior team. He had 13 points in just six games and was named tournament MVP.

Bergeron was able to suit up for Canada as a junior player because NHLers were locked out in 2004–05. He was playing the season in the American Hockey

League when he left for the World Juniors, where he made an impression on young prodigy Sidney Crosby. "I probably asked him about a thousand questions," recalled Crosby. "He was great about it, and we've been friends ever since."

The two have since shared a history of concussions. On October 27, 2007, Bergeron was knocked unconscious and taken from the arena on a stretcher. He played only 10 games in 2007–08 and missed a month in 2008–09 after suffering a second concussion.

Back to full health in 2010 Bergeron added an Olympic gold to his world championship and joined the ultra-exclusive Triple Gold Club with a Stanley Cup ring the following season. He had 20 points in 23 postseason games in 2011, including two goals in Game 7 as the Bruins beat the Vancouver Canucks to win their first championship in 39 years.

Bergeron led the NHL in 2011–12 with a plus-36 rating, was second in faceoff percentage (59.3) and won his first Selke Trophy as the best defensive forward in the league.

In 2013 the Bruins came within two wins of a second Stanley Cup, with Bergeron playing through broken ribs and a punctured lung in the final. Immediately after losing Game 6 and the Cup to the Chicago Blackhawks, he was rushed to the hospital.

"I'd do it again because I had learned from others the sacrifices you need to make as a team in order to win in the playoffs," wrote Bergeron in *The Players' Tribune* in 2017. "I'd do it again because my teammates and I knew what it felt like to hoist the Cup."

Bergeron, who added a second Olympic gold at the 2014 Sochi Games and then three more Selke Trophies in 2014, 2015 and 2017, also became a charter member of the Quadruple Gold Club after winning the 2016 World Cup of Hockey.

The gold standard of two-way centers, Bergeron had as complete a season as possible in 2018–19 and finished top 3 in Selke voting for the eighth straight time. In only 65 games played, including his 1,000th, the 33-year-old tied his career best with 32 goals and set a new high with 79 points. Bergeron was sixth in the NHL in faceoff win percentage (56.6), second in offensive-zone faceoff percentage (59.7) and fifth in power-play faceoff wins (162). He also had a plus-23 rating and led the Bruins in shorthanded goals (4) and shot attempt differential (56.73).

Like in 2013, however, the postseason ended just shy of a Stanley Cup, this time after a Game 7 loss to the St. Louis Blues in the final. Bruins fans were left wondering what might have been if their best player hadn't been fighting through a serious groin injury.

Bergeron called the loss "heartbreaking," but although he didn't deliver another Cup to Boston he did show the young Bruins how the game should be played — with guts, grace, class and integrity.

Won gold at the 2004 World Championship and 2005 World Junior Championship

Won gold at the 2010 and 2014 Olympics

Won the Stanley Cup in 2011

Awarded the Frank J. Selke Trophy four times (2012, 2014, 2015, 2017)

Won the World Cup of Hockey in 2016

NIKITA KUCHEROV

ATLANTIC DIVISION

Lightning | Right Wing | 86

At 13, Lionel Messi was signed by FC Barcelona and brought over from Argentina because the team agreed to pay for his medical treatment when his home side wouldn't — one of the wisest investments in sports history. There are parallels to Nikita Kucherov, who's making his own case as the best on Earth in his chosen sport.

A native of Maykop, in southern Russia, Kucherov started with hand-me-down skates that were three sizes too big but eventually made his way onto CSKA Moscow's youth teams.

As an undersized winger he was lightly regarded by NHL scouts, and even after setting a tournament record with 21 points in seven games at the 2011 Under-18 World Championship, he still lasted into the second round of the draft that year, when he was chosen 58th overall by the Tampa Bay Lightning.

That's when the problems with CSKA began. Kucherov had injuries to both shoulders, but the team didn't believe him and refused to pay for surgery. His agent approached then-Lightning general manager Steve Yzerman days after the draft and he agreed to look after Kucherov's treatment and recovery.

Kucherov decided to void the rest of his contract with CSKA and came over to North America as a 19-year-old in 2012. He spent one year in the Quebec Major Junior Hockey League, splitting it between the Quebec Remparts and Rouyn-Noranda Huskies and earning 63 points in 33 games.

His 2013–14 season started with the Syracuse

Crunch in the American Hockey League, and after 24 points in 17 games Kucherov was called up by the Lightning in November. He scored his first NHL goal on his first shot of his first shift in his first game but spent parts of the season and playoffs learning from the press box.

Playing a full slate of games in 2014–15, Kucherov had 65 points and tied for the NHL lead in plus-minus at plus-38. He added 22 points — including 10 goals — in 26 playoff games to help the Lightning reach the Stanley Cup Final.

After scoring 66 points in 2015–16 Kucherov had 11 goals in 17 playoff games as the Lightning reached Game 7 of the Eastern Conference Final. He was just the third player in NHL history to score 10 or more goals in multiple playoffs before turning 23, joining Jeremy Roenick and Evgeni Malkin.

In 2017–18 Kucherov became the third player in franchise history with 100 points, good for third in the NHL, and he had 17 points in 17 playoff games as the Lightning lost in Game 7 of the Eastern Conference Final again.

In 2018 Kucherov agreed to an eight-year, $76 million contract extension, and Adidas also signed him as a "Creator" — a roster of international musicians, artists and athletes who show how creativity can change a game and the world. "He's a creator in all senses of the word," explained Adidas senior director Dan Near. "He's somebody that does the unexpected, that has his own personality, albeit humble."

The new contracts seem like a bargain after Kucherov's 2018–19 season. His 128 points, which were 12 ahead of Connor McDavid in second, were the highest total of any NHL player since Mario Lemieux in 1995–96 and the most ever by a Russian, breaking the record set by Alexander Mogilny in 1992–93. His 87 assists tied Jaromir Jagr's NHL record for most by a winger in one season.

"His hockey IQ is one of the best I've ever seen," said Pavel Datsyuk, the future Hall of Famer whose photos were on Kucherov's wall growing up. "Hockey fans are fortunate to witness Nikita play the game."

Since his first full season in the NHL, Kucherov is third in the league with 444 points, 47 ahead of Alex Ovechkin in fourth and trailing Patrick Kane by one point and Sidney Crosby by three.

Two days after turning 26, Kucherov swept the 2019 NHL Awards and joined those three future Hall of Famers by winning the Hart Trophy, the Art Ross Trophy and the Ted Lindsay Award.

Now the team-first, pass-first creator just has to join them in his ultimate goal — getting his name etched on hockey's holy grail.

"To me, it doesn't matter how many points I get," said Kucherov after accepting his awards. "The whole thing is about the Stanley Cup. That's why you play the game. You want to win. It doesn't matter about the individual stuff."

Played in three NHL All-Star Games (2017, 2018, 2019)

Won bronze at the 2017 and 2019 World Championship

Holds the single-season record for the most points ever by a Russian player (128)

Won the Hart Trophy, Art Ross Trophy and Ted Lindsay Award in 2019

AUSTON MATTHEWS

No NHL team is more thirsty for success than the Toronto Maple Leafs. For the past 52 years they've been wandering in the championship desert in search of a Stanley Cup. But a savior arrived from Arizona of all places, which is about as far away from Toronto as possible, in hockey terms.

Auston Matthews is a child of the NHL's southern expansion. He was raised by his Mexican mother, Ema, and Californian father, Brian, in Scottsdale, Arizona, where he was seduced by the speed of Coyotes games.

Matthews learned the game on Ozzie Ice, a facility with two small rinks created by pipeline entrepreneur Dwayne Osadchuk. He played countless hours of 3-on-3 with older kids, and the quick, tight games forced him to learn to puckhandle in the proverbial phone booth. He also sharpened his skating under the unorthodox tutelage of Boris Dorozhenko, who fled the Soviet Union to run the Mexican national hockey team. Dorozhenko met Matthews' father because they both spoke Spanish.

At 15 Matthews scored 55 goals and 100 points in 48 games with the AAA Arizona Bobcats, earning him a spot in the U.S. National Team Development Program. He played with the under-18 national team at 16, averaging nearly a point a game.

When Matthews was 17 he continued on the road less traveled, eschewing college or major junior hockey for a year in Europe. Two days shy of being eligible for the 2015 NHL Entry Draft, he chose to play in Zurich for the ZSC Lions in the National League A, Switzerland's top professional circuit.

Playing against men, the 18-year-old Matthews had 24 goals and 46 points in 36 games, the highest totals in league history for a player under 20. He won the Rising Star award and came second in MVP voting.

Meanwhile, in Toronto, the Maple Leafs had finished last in the NHL in 2015–16. The odds and draft lottery balls smiled upon them and they chose Matthews number one overall, their first top pick since they drafted Wendel Clark in 1985.

- Selected first overall in the 2016 NHL Entry Draft
- Scored four goals in his NHL debut, a first in the modern era
- Played in three NHL All-Star Games (2017, 2018, 2019)
- Won the Calder Trophy in 2017

If there was any doubt Matthews could make it at the highest level he erased it in his first NHL game. On October 12, 2016, against the Ottawa Senators, Matthews had the greatest NHL debut in nearly 100 years, becoming the first player in modern NHL history (since 1943–44) to score four goals in his first game. Only Joe Malone of the Montreal Canadiens and Harry Hyland of the Montreal Wanderers had more, both scoring five on December 19, 1917, the very first night of the newly formed NHL.

The rest of the season was a dream for the Maple Leafs and Matthews. On March 7, 2017, he broke Clark's 31-year-old franchise rookie record with his 35th goal of the season, and on April 8 he scored his 40th into an empty net to clinch the Leafs' first playoff berth since 2013.

Matthews is the fourth player in NHL history to score 40 goals in a season before his 20th birthday, and he joined Mats Sundin as the only Leaf in the past 22 years to score at least 40. He also led the league in even-strength goals with 31 and was the only player to record a shot in all 82 games. He capped it all off by winning the Calder Trophy to end the Maple Leafs' Calder dry spell, which had stretched back to Brit Selby in 1966.

A shoulder injury cost Matthews 14 games in 2018–19, but he still had 37 goals and 73 points in 68 games and was named captain of the Atlantic Division at the All-Star Game, his third straight trip to the midseason classic.

Since entering the NHL Matthews is first in 5-on-5 goals with 79, four ahead of Connor McDavid in 30 fewer games played, and fifth in total goals with 111, just one behind McDavid and teammate John Tavares.

Toronto has been eliminated in the first round in each of his three seasons, but with Matthews signed to a five-year, $58.17 million contract, Leafs Nation can at least stop worrying about him decamping for the warm comforts of home in the Arizona desert. Instead they can dream of him ending that other team drought — the one that started in 1967.

VICTOR HEDMAN

When 18-year-old Victor Hedman joined the Tampa Bay Lightning after being drafted second overall in 2009, it was only the second organization he'd ever played in. From the age of 6 he'd played in the legendary MoDo system in his hometown of Ornskoldsvik, Sweden. "Just a good hockey town, rinks everywhere, outdoor and indoor," said Hedman. "You're skating for hours and hours, you go home to eat and then you go out again. Get the lights on when it gets dark. Just all about hockey."

The main employer is the Holmen paper mill, which sponsors MoDo and is where Hedman's dad, Olle, worked when he wasn't managing equipment for the hockey team. A town of just 27,000 people that sits six hours north of Stockholm, Ornskoldsvik has produced NHL stars Markus Naslund, Henrik and

Daniel Sedin, and Hedman's favorite, Peter Forsberg, among many others.

Between organized and impromptu hockey, Hedman learned to skate through his awkward phases as he grew into his 6-foot-6 frame. Gawky growing up, the defenseman is now 223 pounds and one of the smoothest skaters in the NHL.

After winning silver medals with Sweden at the World Juniors in 2008 and 2009 and Rookie of the Year in the Swedish Hockey League in 2009 as a teenager, Hedman made the move to Florida. "It's probably the toughest . . . to come into this league as an 18-year-old defenseman," said Lightning captain Steven Stamkos. "There were some tough years, but we went through tough years as a team."

Tampa Bay reached the Eastern Conference Final in

2011, but Hedman struggled with injuries the following season and the team slipped back. Meanwhile, the Ottawa Senators' Erik Karlsson, a Swede born the same year as Hedman, won the Norris Trophy in 2012.

Hedman made his case for best defenseman in the game in the 2015 playoffs. Averaging 26 minutes a night and shutting down Jonathan Toews in the Stanley Cup Final, Hedman was a strong Conn Smythe candidate, but Tampa Bay fell to the Chicago Blackhawks in six games.

In 2016–17 Hedman led all defensemen with a career-best 56 assists in 79 games. He had career highs in goals (16) and points (72), behind only Brent Burns of the San Jose Sharks among defensemen. He also led the NHL with 29 power-play assists and ranked second with 33 power-play points.

If it wasn't for career seasons by Burns and Karlsson, who joined Hedman as Norris Trophy finalists in 2017, and the fact that the injury-decimated Lightning missed the playoffs, he likely would have been crowned the NHL's best defenseman.

That was remedied the following season. Hedman scored 17 goals in 2017–18, a career high that put him in a three-way tie for first among defensemen. He added 46 assists, while also setting new career bests with a plus-32 rating and an average of 25:51 minutes of ice time a game. He became the first Lightning player to win the Norris and the third Swede, after Karlsson and Nicklas Lidstrom, who won it seven times.

The recognition took some of the sting out of losing for the third time in Game 7 of the Eastern Conference Final, each to the eventual champion. The 2019 playoffs might have been even more heartbreaking, and illuminating. After tying an NHL record with 62 regular-season wins to stroll to the Presidents' Trophy, the Lightning were swept by the Columbus Blue Jackets in the first round.

Hedman was a Norris finalist once again, despite being limited to 70 games. He had 54 points and a plus-24 rating, while leading the team in average ice time (22:46) for the sixth straight season as the Lightning gave up the fifth-fewest goals in the NHL. He suffered an upper-body injury, possibly a concussion, late in the season and had to sit for the final two games of the series.

The absence clearly hurt. "He can make up for a ton of mistakes that happen," said coach Jon Cooper, not to mention that the power-play success rate rose from 19 to 30 percent with Hedman on the ice.

The Lightning's franchise leader in all career offensive categories for defensemen has taken his place in the pantheon of Ornskoldsvik legends. Now his sights are set on hockey's immortals.

"We want a Stanley Cup championship," said Hedman, who admits that the 2015 defeat still gnaws at him. "You're never going to get over a Stanley Cup loss until you win one."

Awarded the Guldpucken (Golden Puck) as Sweden's best hockey player in 2015

Played in the 2017 NHL All-Star Game

Won gold at the 2017 World Championship

Won the Norris Trophy in 2018

SHEA WEBER

Won gold at the 2005 World Junior Championship and 2007 World Championship

Played in six NHL All-Star Games (2009, 2011, 2012, 2015, 2016, 2017)

Won gold at the 2010 and 2014 Olympics

Received the Mark Messier Leadership Award in 2016

Won the World Cup of Hockey in 2016

Shea Weber is not a fan of the spotlight, but that wasn't a problem while he toiled in relative anonymity in Nashville. Yet that all changed with a seismic trade on June 29, 2016.

The Predators dealt Weber to the Montreal Canadiens for P.K. Subban — one with the biggest shot in the NHL, the other with the biggest personality. "I'm not P.K. Subban," said Weber after the trade. "I'm not going to try to be."

Which is why the Canadiens traded for him. Weber, who was the Predators' captain and the 2016 Mark Messier Leadership Award winner, is "quiet, succinct, stoic but polite," according to sports writer Bryan Mullen in *The Tennessean*, "whose slap shots rip twine, break bones and create myths."

That's not an exaggeration. At least four teammates have had bones broken from being hit by a Weber slap shot, and he won the hardest shot at the NHL All-Star Skills Competition three years in a row.

The myth went international when Weber ripped a puck through the twine against Germany at the 2010 Vancouver Olympics, which had to be reviewed in slow motion to be seen and confirmed.

Weber grew up in Sicamous, British Columbia. He inherited his work ethic from his parents, a sawmill worker and a hairdresser, and his intimidating stare came from his mom, Tracy, who died of cancer a few months after seeing her son win Olympic gold in Vancouver.

Between the ages of 14 and 15, Weber shot up from 5-foot-9 to 6-foot-2, but it wasn't enough to convince the Western Hockey League and so he went undrafted. The Kelowna Rockets signed him for the 2001–02 season as a 16-year-old, and the following year he led the team with 167 penalty minutes. The Predators liked his pluck and drafted him in the second round, 49th overall, in 2003.

After winning gold at the World Juniors in 2005, Weber joined the Predators full time for the 2006–07 season. Over the next decade he was Nashville's foundation and one of the game's finest defensemen.

The 6-foot-4, 229-pound safety valve plays up to 30 minutes a night. His 203 goals since entering the league lead all NHL defensemen, and he's finished in the top four in Norris Trophy voting five times.

One year does not a trade make, but Weber won over Habs fans quickly by leading the Canadiens in points and the NHL in plus-minus early in the 2016–17 season, finishing with 42 points and a plus-20 rating in 78 games.

On the day of a provincial election just prior to the 2018–19 season, another decision that impacts almost as many Quebecers was also made in Montreal. Weber, who was still recovering from surgeries on his left foot and right knee, was named the Canadiens' captain. General manager Marc Bergevin called the move "obvious."

After missing nearly a full calendar year Weber came back in December 2018. He made an immediate impact and sparked a strong second half as the Canadiens fell just short of the playoff picture. He finished the season with 14 goals, which tied him for eighth among NHL defensemen — and all but one of the players ahead of him (Kris Letang) had played at least 20 more games.

The Weber-Subban trade will be scrutinized for years to come and the jury might still be out, but Weber played five fewer games than Subban in 2018–19 and had five more goals (14 to nine) and two more points (33 to 31). He was also a calming presence on the back end and the veteran leader of a surprising young team, while rumors of Subban's departure swirled around Nashville by season's end and he was eventually traded to the New Jersey Devils in the off-season. Maybe that's enough to end the debate.

Despite the strength of his individual play, Weber still "burns for the Stanley Cup," according to Blair Robinson, his Junior B coach. In a city that's occasionally set on fire during the playoffs, he fits right in.

CAREY PRICE

Carey Price was born in Vancouver but moved to Anahim Lake, a remote town in central British Columbia, when he was 3. He has Nuxalk and Southern Carrier Indigenous heritage, and his mother, Lynda, is the former chief of the Ulkatcho First Nation and the first woman elected to the Union of BC Indian Chiefs' board of directors.

The goaltending genes came from his father, Jerry, an eighth-round pick of the Philadelphia Flyers in 1978 whose bad knees kept him from reaching the NHL. There were no rinks in Anahim Lake, so Jerry cleared a section of Corkscrew Creek that ran through their property to teach his son.

At 9, Carey had outgrown the creek, but the closest team was in Williams Lake, 200 miles away. After making the eight-hour round trip one too many times, his father bought a small plane to cut down on the commute. Father and son speak fondly of the time spent together on those trips, which ended when Carey moved to Pasco, Washington, at 16 to play for the Tri-City Americans of the Western Hockey League.

Price was the seventh overall pick in the 2002 WHL draft and went fifth overall in the 2005 NHL Entry Draft, despite the Canadiens having a Vezina and Hart Trophy winner in Jose Theodore. Then-general manager Bob Gainey couldn't pass up a "thoroughbred."

After the Americans were eliminated in the 2007 WHL playoffs, Price joined Hamilton for the American Hockey League postseason and posted a .936 save percentage to lead the Bulldogs to the

Calder Cup. It topped a season in which he'd also won gold at the 2007 World Junior Championship. Price became the first goalie to be named Canadian Hockey League Goaltender of the Year, World Juniors MVP and AHL playoff MVP in the same season.

Despite this pedigree Price wasn't anointed Montreal's starter immediately. In 2010 the Canadiens made a surprise run to the Eastern Conference Final thanks to goaltender Jaroslav Halak. Forced to choose between goalies in the off-season, Montreal management traded Halak, to the consternation of many.

In his first preseason as the number one goalie, Price had a shaky start and the fans let him know it. Afterward he counseled them to "relax, chill out."

That kind of calm is particularly helpful when the whole country is watching. At the 2014 Sochi Olympics Price had a 0.59 goals-against average and .972 save percentage in five games — all victories, which included a shutout streak of 164:19 that stretched over the semifinal and gold medal game.

That was merely a prelude to a historic 2014–15 season. Price's league-leading 44 wins broke the franchise record, and he was first in goals-against average (1.96) and save percentage (.933). He won the Hart Trophy, Vezina Trophy and Ted Lindsay Award and shared the William M. Jennings Trophy.

During an acceptance speech, Price said, "I would really like to encourage First Nations youth to be leaders in their communities. Be proud of your heritage and don't be discouraged from the improbable."

Price signed a record eight-year, $84 million contract in 2017 and the Canadiens got their money's worth in 2018–19. He played more minutes than any other goalie (3,880) and almost dragged Montreal into the playoffs, playing 28 of the team's final 30 games. From December 1 to the end of the season he was second in the NHL in wins (28), sixth in goals-against average (2.25) and eighth in save percentage (.925).

Along the way Price passed Jacques Plante for the most wins in Canadiens' history, finishing the season with 321, and was voted best goalie in the league by his peers in an NHLPA poll.

A role model for youth, Price had an impact off the ice as well. In February 2019, ahead of a game in Toronto, Price eased the grief of 11-year-old Anderson Whitehead, who had just lost his mother to cancer. He met the tearful youngster after practice and gave him two signed sticks as well as a long hug.

"It's the happiest I've ever been in my life," said Whitehead. "I always hoped it was going to happen. My mom always said it could happen."

Anderson's tears were joy and relief according to his father, Kevin. "The weight and the anger that he's been carrying around, all that stuff — there are no words to say thank you."

Value isn't always measured in dollars and cents.

Won gold at the 2007 World Junior Championship

Won gold at the 2014 Olympics and named best goaltender

Won the Hart Trophy, Vezina Trophy, Ted Lindsay Award and William M. Jennings Trophy in 2015

Won the World Cup of Hockey in 2016

Holds the franchise record for most wins by a Canadiens goalie (321 and counting)

BRAD MARCHAND

Long known as the Little Ball of Hate, he's now one of the NHL's top point producers. And when it comes to Brad Marchand, you can't have the latter without the former.

Having made a name for himself as a trouble-maker before he was a scorer, Marchand's moniker even caught the attention of a U.S. president. When Marchand was at the White House with his Boston Bruins teammates after winning the 2011 Stanley Cup, Barack Obama asked, "What's up with that nickname, man?" For once, Marchand was left speechless. "It really caught me off guard," he said.

The nickname was inherited from former NHLer Pat Verbeek, who had 522 career goals and nearly 3,000 penalty minutes, but Marchand has been given plenty of his own. He's been called Squirrel, Weapon of Mass Distraction, Rat, Pigeon, Brat and Nose Face Killah. His first was Tomahawk, thanks to a two-handed swing that dented an opponent's facemask when he was a 14-year-old in Lower Sackville, Nova Scotia.

Rob O'Brien was in the stands scouting for his Dartmouth Subways major midget team when Marchand took batting practice on his opponent's face. It convinced him to recruit the undersized for-ward. "I really felt that his temperament could be an asset rather than a detriment. Brad is a real personality on the ice. A lot of coaches tried to beat that out of him, but I encouraged it. I thought it was fantastic that he was able to do it. I used it to his advantage."

After running roughshod with his midget team,

Marchand was a second-round pick of the Moncton Wildcats in the 2004 Quebec Major Junior Hockey League draft. In 2006 Moncton reached the Memorial Cup final and soon after Boston drafted Marchand in the third round, 71st overall.

Marchand played two more seasons in junior, split between the Val-d'Or Foreurs and the Halifax Mooseheads, and won back-to-back gold medals at the World Juniors in 2007 and 2008 before turning pro.

In 2010–11, his first full season in Boston, Marchand came as advertised and helped the Bruins win their first Stanley Cup since 1972. He had 11 goals in 25 playoff games, a Bruins rookie playoff record, and the team was 9-0 in games that he scored. He had five goals in the last five games against the Vancouver Canucks in the Stanley Cup Final, and he also punched Canucks star Daniel Sedin in the jaw six times when the Bruins had Game 6 in hand. When asked why afterward, he replied, "Because I felt like it."

Marchand was penalized but escaped suspension. He scored two goals in the decisive seventh game, and he's been beloved in Beantown ever since.

In 2015–16 Marchand had 37 goals and a team-leading plus-21 rating. It earned him a spot on Team Canada for the 2016 World Championship, where he won gold. A few months later, he represented his country at the World Cup of Hockey. Playing alongside Sidney Crosby and Boston teammate Patrice Bergeron on Canada's top line, he led the tournament with five goals in six games, including the winning goal in the final, a shorthanded tally with less than a minute remaining.

His confidence buoyed, Marchand challenged for the NHL lead in goals and points in 2016–17, prompting Hart Trophy buzz. He finished tied for fourth in goals (39) and fifth in points (85), both career highs.

After another 85-point season in 2017–18, Marchand took it to another level in 2018–19, tying Crosby for fifth in scoring at an even 100 points, including a career-high 64 assists. In the postseason he was fueled by his usual antics, getting dangerously close to the line and then gleefully leaping over it. He sucker punched the Columbus Blue Jackets' Scott Harrington in the back of the head in the second round but avoided disciplinary action again, despite being suspended six times for a total of 19 games in his career.

Marchand went on to equal Conn Smythe Trophy winner Ryan O'Reilly for first in playoff scoring with 23 points, but the Bruins lost to the St. Louis Blues in the Stanley Cup Final.

Some took great delight in sharing images of Marchand crying on the ice and in the dressing room after the Game 7 loss at home, an example of his passion for winning and the divine retribution of hockey gods all at once. When you make that many enemies you're bound to become a meme.

Won gold at the 2007 and 2008 World Junior Championship

Won the Stanley Cup in 2011

Won gold at the 2016 World Championship

Won the World Cup of Hockey in 2016

Played in two NHL All-Star Games (2017, 2018)

STEVEN STAMKOS

ATLANTIC DIVISION
Lightning | Center | 91

A t the age of 29 Steven Stamkos is already a veteran of 11 NHL seasons, and in 2018–19 he passed Vincent Lecavalier for a new Tampa Bay Lightning record in career goals. Stamkos' 393, many from his nearly unstoppable one-timer, trail only Alex Ovechkin since he made his NHL debut, but he's had more than his share of lows.

The first overall pick in 2008 by the Lightning has lived up to his lofty status as one of the most natural goal-scorers of his generation, but he's lost large swaths of his prime to injury.

Growing up in Unionville, Ontario, Stamkos started skating at 2 years old and played hockey with future NHL stars P.K. Subban and John Tavares. Stamkos and Tavares played on a summer team together that went 50 games with only one defeat, which Stamkos blames on reverse-favoritism. His father was the coach, but instead of sending out his son for the shootout he chose Tavares, who missed his attempt and cost them their unblemished record.

The two good friends became the second and third players, after Eric Lindros, to be drafted first overall in both the Ontario Hockey League and NHL. Tavares was drafted a year earlier in the OHL because he'd been granted exceptional player status, but Stamkos preceded him by a year in the NHL draft.

Stamkos earned his selection with big numbers for the Sarnia Sting, and he was also named the OHL's Scholastic Player of the Year. "He was an excellent student, an honor roll student. I could tell you that the teachers at our school were amazed at this kid," recalled Paul Titanic, Stamkos' coach on the Markham Waxers and gym teacher at St. Brother André Catholic School in Markham.

Stamkos made a good first impression in the NHL too. He won the Maurice Richard Trophy in his second season after leading the league with 51 goals in 2009–10. The following season he helped the Lightning reach the playoffs for the first time in four years, where they lost the Eastern Conference Final in seven games to the Boston Bruins.

- Won gold at the 2008 World Junior Championship
- Selected first overall in the 2008 NHL Entry Draft
- Won the Maurice Richard Trophy twice (2010, 2012)
- Played in six NHL All-Star Games (2010, 2012, 2015, 2016, 2018, 2019)
- Won the World Cup of Hockey in 2016

After dipping slightly to 45 goals in 2010–11, Stamkos took home his second "Rocket" Richard award the following season after becoming just the second player since 1996 to score 60 goals.

Stamkos was skating smoothly toward Hall of Fame credentials, but injuries began taking their toll in 2013–14 after he fractured the tibia in his right leg and missed 45 games. He returned on March 6, 2014, skating out for the first time as the captain of the Lightning, the 10th in franchise history.

After playing the full 82 games in 2014–15 and scoring 43 goals, Stamkos and the Lightning reached the Stanley Cup Final, losing in six games to the Chicago Blackhawks.

Tampa Bay was anticipating another long playoff run in 2015–16 when Stamkos was shut down with blood clots in his shoulder late in the season. He had a rib removed to alleviate the problem and made an inspiring but ultimately futile comeback in Game 7 of the conference final against Pittsburgh.

In a disturbing déjà vu, Stamkos had nine goals and 20 points in 17 games before tearing the lateral meniscus in his right knee in November 2016. He had surgery and missed the remainder of the season. Emotionally it was Stamkos' most difficult injury. "You just feel for him because you know how much he wants to play," said Lightning coach Jon Cooper.

The franchise cornerstone was back to health and form in 2018–19, playing every game for the first time in four years. His 45 goals were fourth in the NHL, and his 98 points set a new career high. But disappointment still followed.

The Lightning had 62 wins and 128 points, 21 ahead of the second overall Calgary Flames, and they boasted the first trio of 40-plus goal-scorers (Stamkos, Nikita Kucherov and Brayden Point) since the 1995–96 Penguins, so it was stunning when the Columbus Blue Jackets swept them in the first round.

"This group is not chasing regular-season titles," said Stamkos bluntly, calling the season a failure after he had just a goal and an assist in the series, both in the last game. "We want a Stanley Cup championship."

In a decorated career with its fair share of disappointments, it may have been his lowest point.

JOHN TAVARES

John Tavares is the National Lacrosse League's all-time leading scorer; his nephew John Tavares is a pretty decent athlete himself.

The younger John was so talented that he became the first player to be granted exceptional player status by the Ontario Hockey League at just 14. The native of Mississauga, Ontario, was then selected first overall in the 2005 OHL draft by the Oshawa Generals.

In his rookie year Tavares had 45 goals and 77 points to win both the OHL and Canadian Hockey League Rookie of the Year awards. In his second year he had 72 goals and 134 points, breaking Wayne Gretzky's record for goals by a 16-year-old and taking home the OHL's Most Outstanding Player and CHL's Player of the Year awards.

The Islanders took Tavares first overall in 2009, and in 2011–12 he had 81 points in 82 games, becoming the fourth under-21 player in franchise history to score at least 73 points. The other three — Mike Bossy, Bryan Trottier and Denis Potvin — are all Hall of Famers.

In 2013 Tavares was named the 14th captain in team history. He was a no-brainer for Team Canada at the 2014 Sochi Olympics; however, in a game against Latvia he tore ligaments in his left knee. He won gold while on the injured reserve but was lost for the rest of the NHL season.

After a full recovery prior to 2014–15, Tavares had his best season to date. He finished second in the NHL with 86 points and was named a Hart Trophy finalist.

Tavares spread more joy to Isles fans in the 2016 playoffs. He had the tying goal in the last minute of Game 6 against the Florida Panthers and scored in double overtime to clinch the series. It was the first time the Islanders had reached the second round since 1993, and Tavares was the first player in their illustrious playoff history to score the tying goal in the final minute of regulation and the winner in overtime.

But the flipside of great joy is great pain, and there's far more of the latter in sports. Tavares became one of the most sought-after free agents in NHL history in 2018, and after a courtship by six teams he chose to sign a seven-year, $77 million contract with the Toronto Maple Leafs, thrilling his hometown and breaking the hearts of Long Islanders. After watching their captain of five years reach fifth on the franchise's all-time scoring list, they lost him for nothing.

Tavares announced his decision on Twitter by posting a picture of himself as a child sleeping in Maple Leafs pajamas. It was fodder for Islanders fans when Toronto paid a visit to Nassau Coliseum in February 2019, his first game back. "Pajama Boy" was one of the only insults fit for print as the pumped-up crowd vented about their former savior.

The Islanders got their revenge on the scoreboard with a 6–1 win, but Tavares said all the right things, and if he was bothered by the response he kept it well hidden. There's no lack of passion on the ice, but he is a hockey automaton, a relentless machine who was groomed for stardom from an early age.

The Islanders were the surprise of the NHL in 2018–19 and reached the second round of the playoffs while the Leafs were out in the first, providing the former's fan base with a little schadenfreude.

The Maple Leafs had no buyer's remorse, however. Tavares lived up to his hype in his first season in Toronto, finishing with 88 points in 82 games. His 47 goals were third in the NHL and nine more than his previous career high. They were the most by a player in his first year with the Maple Leafs and the highest season total since Dave Andreychuk's 53 in 1993–94. Tavares also broke Darryl Sittler's franchise record for goals by a center.

"He scores greasy ones, he scores nice ones, works hard down low, he makes plays and can really do it all," said teammate and team leader Morgan Rielly. "When you watch him work the way he does and grind the way he does — but also have his skill — it's pretty to watch."

Only two players have now scored more goals than Tavares' 319 since he was drafted: Alex Ovechkin and Steven Stamkos. He's seventh in points (709) in the span, but Toronto also got more than pure scoring power.

"He treats his job very seriously. He's a good role model for us," added Rielly. "The best part about him is what he does off the ice. That's been a pleasure to watch."

Won the 2009 World Junior Championship and named tournament MVP

Played in six NHL All-Star Games (2012, 2015, 2016, 2017, 2018, 2019)

Voted a Hart Trophy finalist twice (2013, 2015)

Won gold at the 2014 Olympics

Won the World Cup of Hockey in 2016

MORGAN RIELLY

Growing up in West Vancouver, Morgan Rielly was one of those kids who could pick up any sport and excel immediately.

When he outgrew the local hockey system at 14 he moved to Wilcox, Saskatchewan, to play at hockey factory Notre Dame, where he captained the team to a national title. Rielly then went to Moose Jaw to play for the Warriors, who took him second overall in the Western Hockey League draft in 2009. In his second season he was ranked as high as second by NHL Central Scouting, but he tore his ACL and played only 18 games.

"I've never seen a young man work that hard on rehab," said Warriors general manager Alan Millar. "He wanted back in the lineup. He wanted to win a championship. That's a credit to him and his character and leadership. It didn't take me very long to realize that he was pretty special, both on and off the ice."

The Toronto Maple Leafs were undeterred by the injury and took Rielly fifth overall in 2012. Then-general manager Brian Burke couldn't pass up the swift, creative defenseman.

After being drafted Rielly went back to Moose Jaw and scored 12 goals and 54 points, good for third and fifth, respectively, among WHL defensemen. He then finished the year playing 14 regular-season and five playoff games for the Toronto Marlies in the American Hockey League.

In 2013–14, at 19, Rielly stuck with the Maple Leafs and proved himself mature beyond his years. He played 73 games and was second among rookie defensemen in assists (25) and sixth in points (27).

Expectations were high in Toronto for the 6-foot-1, 221-pound Rielly, and over the course of two more bleak years he was often the team's best player. Then a regime change brought Brendan Shanahan and Lou Lamoriello to Toronto's front office and Mike Babcock behind the bench. Luck and savvy drafting gave the roster William Nylander, Mitch Marner and Auston Matthews in 2016–17. Suddenly, at 22,

- Selected second overall in the 2009 WHL draft and fifth overall in the 2012 NHL Entry Draft
- Won gold at the 2012 Hlinka Gretzky Cup
- Won gold at the 2016 World Championship and named one of Canada's top three players
- Led all NHL defensemen with 20 goals in 2018–19

Rielly had become a veteran on one of the youngest, most exciting teams in the NHL.

In March 2017 Rielly turned 23 and played his 300th NHL game, and a few weeks later the Leafs clinched the first playoff berth of his NHL career. Their prize was the Washington Capitals, and the young Leafs took them to six games, five of which went to overtime.

"You learn more from the tough times than you do from the good times, and I think it's good to go through these things when you are young," said Rielly. "It's a bit of an eye-opener and it's not all going to be easy."

It certainly hasn't been for Rielly and his team. They have become a regular-season powerhouse but followed that playoff baptism with two more first-round losses, both in seven games to the Boston Bruins.

Rielly, meanwhile, has transformed into one of the team's leaders. When asked about teammate Jake Gardiner, the object of much scorn after the 2019

elimination game, Rielly cursed on *Hockey Night in Canada* in defense of his fellow defenseman. To stand up to the media and for his teammates after a heartbreaking loss is the kind of character that earns respect.

Rielly is now 25 and in his prime. He's missed only 22 career games and in 2018–19 he led all NHL defensemen with 20 goals and was third among blueliners in scoring with 72 points. He's just the third Toronto defenseman to have 70 points in a season, after Borje Salming and Ian Turnbull, and the first to score 20 goals since Al Iafrate in 1989–90.

Rielly was also a plus-24 while playing more than 23 minutes a night. He spent only 14 minutes in the penalty box all season despite defending against the opponents' top players. They're the kind of numbers that usually earn a Norris Trophy nomination.

Nicknamed the Chosen One in junior, the ego-free and unassuming Rielly has become the elite defenseman the Maple Leafs have long coveted with the personality to thrive in the fishbowl atmosphere of Toronto.

KEITH YANDLE

With an abundance of confidence and talent, Keith Yandle had options when he graduated from high school.

Yandle had 14 goals and 54 points in 34 games in his final year at Cushing Academy, a prep school in Ashburnham, Massachusetts. His efforts caught the eye of the Phoenix (now Arizona) Coyotes, who selected him in the fourth round of the 2005 NHL Entry Draft.

Not ready to jump straight to the pros for the 2005–06 season Yandle was instead hoping to finish high school a year early so that he could join his older brother, Brian, who was entering his final season at the University of New Hampshire. "It was a big decision," said Keith. "I wanted to go play university with my brother. It didn't pan out that way. I wasn't able to move up a grade to go play with him."

Yandle, who was born in Boston and raised just south in Milton, did become a Wildcat, just not a UNH one. While his brother played his senior year, Keith went across the border to play for Moncton in the Quebec Major Junior Hockey League.

In 2005–06 Yandle had 25 goals, 84 points and a plus-50 rating in 66 games. He won the Emile "Butch" Bouchard Trophy as the QMJHL's best defenseman and was named Canadian Hockey League Defenseman of the Year. With future Boston Bruin Brad Marchand, the Wildcats captured the QMJHL title and a trip to the Memorial Cup, where Yandle had three goals in five games.

Yandle spent the next two seasons bouncing between

the Coyotes and their American Hockey League affiliate in San Antonio. Then toward the end of Yandle's first full season in the NHL, Coyotes coach Wayne Gretzky made Yandle a healthy scratch on March 22, 2009. It was the last time Yandle would sit and watch. He played every game over the next decade, including 84 in 2014–15 because of a midseason trade.

On March 1, 2015, after 558 games and 311 points in a Coyotes uniform, Yandle was dealt to the New York Rangers. With unrestricted free agency looming in the summer of 2016 he was then shipped to the Florida Panthers and signed a seven-year, $44.45 million contract three days later.

In his third season in Florida, at the age of 32, Yandle had a career year. He set career highs in assists (53) and points (62) in 2018–19, which were fourth and fifth among NHL defensemen.

Yandle's 39 power-play points set a single-season Panthers record, led all NHL defensemen and were third overall. They helped the Panthers to a franchise-high 26.8 percent success rate on the power play, good for second in the NHL.

A quarterback from the blue line with a cannon of a shot, Yandle also has a gambler's mentality. "Sometimes you've got to beat a guy first before you make the first pass, and sometimes you get in trouble doing it," said teammate Aaron Ekblad. "Whenever he gets in trouble, he weaves his way out of it pretty well. Some kind of crazy saucer pass, no-look, behind his back."

Ekblad was responsible for nearly ending the ironman streak when his slap shot hit his teammate in the foot in December 2016, but Yandle soldiered on and stretched it to 797 consecutive games played by the end of 2018–19, the fifth longest in NHL history.

"I like the cold tub after a game, glass of scotch, that's about it," Yandle responded, possibly even seri-ously, when asked what the secret to his longevity is.

The locker room cut-up is also the de facto tour guide for his teammates on the road, especially the ones experiencing new cities for the first time. He prefers the culture and restaurants of any given road trip destination to hotel life.

"My biggest claim to fame in the NHL," said Yandle, "is that I've never had room service."

There might be a bit more to his career than that. Since becoming a regular in 2008–09, Yandle is third among NHL defensemen with 514 points, behind only Norris Trophy winners Erik Karlsson and Brent Burns.

Yandle grew up idolizing Ray Bourque, who won five Norris Trophies with Boston and retired after 22 NHL seasons and 1,612 games, winning the Stanley Cup with the Colorado Avalanche in his final year.

They're worthy goals for Yandle. He reached the 900-game plateau in his 11th full season, 2018–19, and at this rate won't need another 11 to eclipse Bourque in games played. Panthers fans just hope Yandle won't have to leave town for the championship.

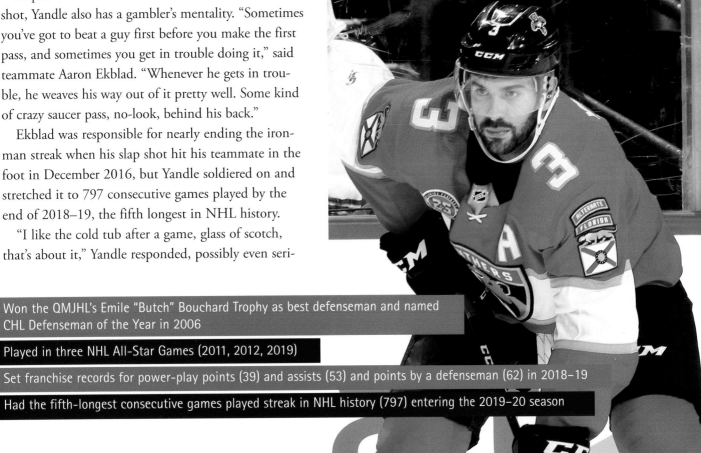

Won the QMJHL's Emile "Butch" Bouchard Trophy as best defenseman and named CHL Defenseman of the Year in 2006

Played in three NHL All-Star Games (2011, 2012, 2019)

Set franchise records for power-play points (39) and assists (53) and points by a defenseman (62) in 2018–19

Had the fifth-longest consecutive games played streak in NHL history (797) entering the 2019–20 season

ANDREI VASILEVSKIY

- Won gold at the 2014 World Championship
- Played in two NHL All-Star Games (2018, 2019)
- Led the NHL in wins in 2018–19 (39) and tied for the lead in 2017–18 (44)
- Won the Vezina Trophy in 2019

Hockey is a family affair for Andrei Vasilevskiy. His older brother, Alexei, is a defenseman with Avtomobilist Yekaterinburg in the Kontinental Hockey League, and his father, Andrei Sr., was a goalie in the old Superleague's second division who backed up Alexander Tyjnych, himself the backup for legend Vladislav Tretiak on the Soviet team.

That connection got Andrei Jr. his first agent. "He was one of those guys who could eat hockey, sleep hockey, breathe hockey," said Tyjnych, who signed Vasilevskiy when he was 15. "My first impression was he had the [guts]. He had the drive to be the best goalie in the world."

Ten years later, Vasilevskiy is there.

A native of Tyumen, Russia, Vasilevskiy was the first goalie taken in the 2012 draft when the Tampa Bay Lightning chose him 19th overall. He remained in Russia for the next two years and made his mark on the international stage. First he led Russia to bronze medals at the 2013 and 2014 World Juniors, with a goals-against average under 2.00 and a save percentage over .930 in both tournaments. Then at the 2014 World Championship in Belarus he allowed only one goal in his two starts with the senior team as the Russians won gold. He was given Russia's Order of Honor as a result.

Having accomplished all he could at home Vasilevskiy left Russia for the Syracuse Crunch, Tampa Bay's American Hockey League affiliate, and made his NHL debut in December 2014. By the end of the season he made history by becoming the first goalie to earn his first NHL playoff victory in relief in the Stanley Cup Final since the New York Rangers' Lester Patrick in 1928. He took over when Ben Bishop was injured in Game 2 of the 2015 final, just his 19th appearance in the NHL.

"He was just cool, not jittery, not arrogant, [but] self-assured, like 'This is where I'm supposed to be,'" said analyst and former NHL goalie Kevin Weekes of Vasilevskiy's Stanley Cup debut.

Vasilevskiy started Game 4, in what was ultimately

a six-game series loss to the Chicago Blackhawks, and replaced an injured Bishop again in the 2016 Eastern Conference Final, taking the eventual champion Pittsburgh Penguins to seven games.

In 2016–17 the Lightning sent the 6-foot-7, 215-pound Bishop to the Los Angeles Kings at the 2017 trade deadline. The 6-foot-4, 215-pound Vasilevskiy was their present and future.

The Lightning's faith in Vasilevskiy was rewarded in 2017–18. He had a 44-17-3 record, tied for most wins with Connor Hellebuyck, and posted a 2.62 goals-against average and a .920 save percentage. He also tied Vezina Trophy winner Pekka Rinne for the league lead in shutouts with eight.

In 2018–19 Vasilevskiy led the NHL with 39 wins, despite missing 14 games with a broken foot, while being fourth with a .925 save percentage and fifth with a 2.40 goals-against average. He was first in the NHL in actual versus expected goals per game and

saved nearly one goal per game (0.94) compared to the league average. After finishing third in Vezina voting the previous year, Vasilevskiy won the award convincingly in 2019 over second-place Bishop.

The Lightning's first-round sweep by the Columbus Blue Jackets was especially shocking considering Vasilevskiy lost back-to-back games only once in the regular season, in a shootout and then in overtime, and finished 13-0-1 after a loss. But the template for their downfall might have been laid early in the season, when the team's run-and-gun style put too much pressure on their goalie.

"Basically we were scoring our way out of trouble," said coach Jon Cooper. "At that moment, put yourself in the shoes of your goaltender. If he's going to have to be our best player every night, we'll be in trouble."

On most nights, on the team that tied the NHL record for most wins in a season in 2018–19, Vasilevskiy is.

ALEKSANDER BARKOV

ATLANTIC DIVISION | Panthers | Center

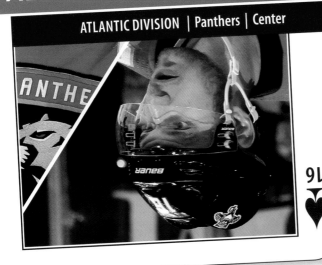

finished ninth in league scoring, one spot behind teammate and former NHLer Ville Nieminen, another Tampere native. Nieminen played alongside father and son on Tappara and says Aleksander got the best of both Russian and Finnish hockey.

"Everything looked professional," said Nieminen. "All his moves, hockey IQ. He's the best student of the game I've ever seen."

The Florida Panthers saw it too and made Barkov the second overall selection behind Nathan MacKinnon in the 2013 NHL draft, ahead of Seth Jones, who was widely assumed to be the number two pick.

It was an unexpected and prescient move, and once again Barkov set the bar for pre-cociousness. He made his NHL debut on October 3, 2013, at the age of 18 years and 31 days old, and became the youngest player to score an NHL goal since Don Raleigh of the New York Rangers in 1943.

Barkov's rookie season was derailed by a knee injury he sustained at the 2014 Olympics, which cost him 24 games. The injury bug continued to bite him over the next three seasons, as back, hand and wrist injuries knocked him out of the lineup for a total of 48 games.

Barkov finally had a healthy season in 2017–18, and it showed on the scoresheet as well as in league-wide recognition. He had 27 goals and 78 points in 79 games, played in the All-Star Game and led the NHL with five shorthanded goals. He finished third in voting for the Lady Byng Trophy and fourth for the Frank J. Selke Trophy.

Then just prior to the 2018–19 season, two weeks after turning 23, the 6-foot-3, 213-pound centerman was named captain of the Panthers.

"He has all of the qualities of a great leader," said general manager Dale Tallon. "Unrivaled work ethic, wisdom beyond his years and the respect and admiration of his teammates. Aleksander's determination and

Alexander Barkov was 29 when he left his home in the former Soviet Union to go to Tampere, Finland, to play for Tappara. It's where his son, Aleksander, was born and it's the city that gave the NHL Teppo Numminen, Jyrki Lumme and Patrik Laine.

It's also where the younger Barkov made his professional debut on October 1, 2011, at the age of 16 years and 29 days old and became the youngest player in Liiga history to earn a point. A few months later he became the youngest player to wear a Finland jersey at the World Juniors and the youngest Finn to score a goal at the tournament.

In the second of his two seasons with Tappara's senior team, Barkov had 48 points in 53 games. He

passion for the game have made him one of the NHL's best and most complete players."

It proved to be another wise choice by the Panthers. Barkov finished 10th in the NHL with 96 points, and he scored one of the highlights of the NHL season: a between-the-legs top-shelf goal that was part of a hat trick against the Montreal Canadiens.

Playing all 82 games, Barkov broke Pavel Bure's 19-year-old franchise record for points in a season and won the Lady Byng after taking only eight minutes in penalties.

In an NHLPA poll during the season, Barkov was voted the fifth-best forward and the most underrated player in the game by his peers. A quiet guy who is happier to lead by example, he's okay with being out of the spotlight.

"He doesn't care for attention, but he does care about this game, this team and about winning games. The rest of it, he does not need," according to team-mate Vincent Trocheck. "He is one of the best hockey players in the world, but all he wants to do is help out his team."

And that means bringing the first NHL championship to Sunrise, Florida.

"I have set my goals here and the first one is to win the Stanley Cup," said Barkov.

Team owner Vinnie Viola believes Barkov is the right man to do it, and not just because his six-year, $35.4 million contract is one of the biggest bargains in the NHL.

"He is the heart and soul of the franchise," said Viola. "He is everything you want to build a Stanley Cup champion around."

Won bronze at the 2014 Olympics

Won silver at the 2016 World Championship

Played in the 2018 NHL All-Star Game

Won the Lady Byng Trophy in 2019

JACK EICHEL

ATLANTIC DIVISION | Sabres | Center

England, then in the East, then in the U.S. When he got to be 15, you knew he was one of the best his age in the whole world — a transcendent player."

The next step for Eichel was joining the U.S. National Team Development Program in Ann Arbor, Michigan. It was a difficult move for the homebody, who was only in his sophomore year of high school, but one that paid off for U.S. hockey and Eichel's career.

In 2013, at the age of 16, Eichel led the U.S. to a bronze medal at the World Under-17 Hockey Challenge and a silver medal at the Under-18 World Championship.

In 2014 he was the Americans' youngest player at the World Junior Championship in Sweden, where he had five points in five games. Eichel was named captain for the 2015 World Juniors and finished his season at the World Championship, where he was the third-leading scorer on a bronze medal–winning team full of NHL players.

Eichel's collegiate hockey was played about 35 miles from home at Boston University. It was a brief but glorious time with the Terriers; he played one season, scoring 26 goals and 71 points in 40 games to lead the nation and become the second freshman ever to win the Hobey Baker Award as the best collegiate player in America.

As the NHL draft approached there was a made-for-TV rivalry between Eichel and Connor McDavid, the most sought-after junior player since Sidney Crosby. The two had crossed paths in international competition a few times but didn't really know each other.

The Edmonton Oilers won the lottery and took McDavid, while the Buffalo Sabres happily chose Eichel second. He scored his first NHL goal in his first game; at 18 years and 345 days he was the youngest Sabre in history to score. Eichel led the Sabres with 24 goals in his rookie season, and he was second among all rookies in both goals and assists behind Artemi Panarin.

In most NHL entry drafts, Jack Eichel would've been the number one pick. The 6-foot-2, 200-pound center with vision, reach, patience and a cannon of a shot is the kind of player a team is built around. But 2015 was not most years.

Growing up in North Chelmsford, Massachusetts, Eichel wanted to play hockey at 4 years old, but he couldn't sign up for the local league until he was 5. So his parents, Bob and Anne, decided to register him in a league in New Hampshire instead of waiting.

"Jack was one of the best players as soon as he joined us," said Chris Masters, who coached Eichel with the Boston Junior Bruins. "But at 10 he started to separate from even the best kids. He became one of the top kids his age in Massachusetts, then in New

Prior to his second NHL season, Eichel was a member of the 23-and-under Team North America at the World Cup of Hockey. Full of confidence after an impressive 2-1 record versus the best in the world, Eichel suffered a serious left ankle sprain in a scrimmage during Buffalo's training camp and missed the first 21 games of the 2016–17 season. It was a blow for a team that was relying on him to lead them back to the playoffs for the first time since 2011.

Eichel missed 15 more games in 2017–18 after spraining his right ankle. He had 10 goals and 29 points in 29 games after coming back, and while facing the strongest opposing players his possession numbers and goals-for percentage were strong.

After a year without a captain, the Sabres anointed Eichel leader prior to the 2018–19 season, which was also the first of his eight-year, $80 million contract. He had 28 goals, 54 assists and 82 points, all career highs, and played in 77 games.

Eichel was the first Sabre with an 80-point season since 2007–08, and with an improvement on his paltry 9.2 percent shooting percentage he would've been flirting with 40 goals and 100 points.

Despite Eichel's heroics the Sabres had a dreadful second half and missed the playoffs for the eighth straight year, the longest active streak in the NHL. It's a fact not lost on Eichel.

"Our fans deserve more," said Eichel. "There were glimpses of some really, really awesome stuff this year . . . It's a city that loves us and they care so much."

Captained the U.S. at the 2015 World Junior Championship

Won the Hobey Baker Award in 2015

Selected second overall in the 2015 NHL Entry Draft

Named to the NHL All-Rookie Team in 2016

Played in two NHL All-Star Games (2018, 2019)

71

DYLAN LARKIN

ATLANTIC DIVISION | Red Wings | Center

The Township of Waterford, Michigan, is about 35 miles northwest of Detroit's Little Caesars Arena. Calling itself Lakeland Paradise, it's a shinny player's dream, with 35 lakes for 75,000 citizens. It's where Hall of Famer Pat LaFontaine grew up and where Dylan Larkin cut his hockey teeth.

"Just me and a puck and a net," remembered Larkin. "That was my childhood. Up here [in the NHL], you want to put up points and win, but there it's just about hockey."

After Larkin's 17 goals and 26 points in 26 games during his second season with the U.S. National Team Development Program, the Red Wings made the local kid the 15th overall pick in 2014, their highest selection since 1991, a reflection of the team's success.

After being drafted Larkin had 15 goals and 47 points in 35 games for the University of Michigan in 2014–15 and was named the Big Ten freshman of the year. He had impressed Team USA brass at the 2015 World Juniors earlier in the year, so after his only season as a Wolverine he was added to the U.S. roster at the World Championship. There the 19-year-old helped the Americans shut out the host Czech Republic 3–0 to win bronze.

Not done yet Larkin joined the Grand Rapids Griffins, Detroit's American Hockey League affiliate, midway through the play-offs and had three goals and five points in six games — his only stint in the minors.

The Red Wings have a history of bringing young players along slowly, but Larkin forced them to make an exception. He had a goal and an assist in his NHL debut in 2015–16, making him the first teen to score for the team since Red Wings legend and general manager Steve Yzerman in 1983.

Larkin had 23 goals and 45 points in his rookie year and made the 2016 NHL All-Star Game, where he set a record for fastest skater at 13.172 seconds around the rink in the skills competition. He suffered a bit of a sophomore slump in 2016–17, and the Red Wings failed to qualify for the postseason for the first time in 25 straight seasons. But it allowed Larkin to play at the 2017 World Championship, where he had 10 points in eight games.

Moving from Henrik Zetterberg's wing to center, Larkin set career highs with 47 assists and 63 points in 2017–18. When Zetterberg retired at the end of the season Larkin took over as the team's number one center and continued his ascent to elite status. His 73 points in 2018–19 tied his friend and fellow superstar center Auston Matthews of the Toronto Maple Leafs as well as Vegas Golden Knights star Mark Stone. He played in all situations and was second on the team in

ice time at 21:51, just eight seconds behind defenseman Danny DeKeyser and ninth among all NHL forwards.

"The number one thing is his inner drive is off the charts," according to Red Wings coach Jeff Blashill. "He's got the inner drive that the great players have. He wants to be great and he wants us to win. He's self-accountable — there are times he gets frustrated, there are times he looks back and he knows he has to be better. So he is self-accountable and he's got great inner drive. Those are great qualities to have as a leader."

Larkin also achieved the exceedingly rare trifecta of leading his team in goals (32), assists (41) and penalty minutes (75). The closest anyone's come in recent memory is Sidney Crosby in his rookie year of 2005–06, but he was still third on his team in the penalty minute category.

Although there's scant record of Gordie Howe actu-ally doing this, having a goal, an assist and a fight in one game became known as the "Gordie Howe hat trick." It's a nod to the Red Wing legend's multi-faceted game and history of stuffing the whole stat sheet.

Detroit fans have now witnessed the birth of the modern season-long equivalent, in which pugilism has been replaced with penalty minutes, to be known as the Dylan Larkin hat trick. Or maybe it should be called the Waterford Whammy.

Won gold at the 2014 Under-18 World Championship
Won bronze at the 2015 and 2018 World Championship
Set a record for fastest skater at the 2016 NHL All-Star Game Skills Competition
Played in the 2016 NHL All-Star Game

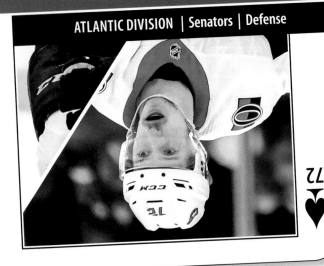

THOMAS CHABOT

ATLANTIC DIVISION | Senators | Defense

hockey world on fire.

At the 2017 World Juniors Chabot led all blue-liners in goals (four) and points (10) and all players in average ice time (26:14). He was named the tournament's best defenseman and won the MVP award, the first blue-liner ever.

Despite losing to Team USA in a shootout for the gold, Canada's alternate captain was the player of the game after skating for 43:53 minutes, including 11:06 in the 20-minute overtime, with a goal and an assist.

"He was great, he was dominant," said head coach Dominique Ducharme. "He was good offensively and defensively, shutting down the best players on the other side. He was just tremendous all tournament. He was a great leader for us."

Chabot finished the 2016–17 QMJHL season with 45 points in 34 games, matching his point total from the year prior in 13 fewer games and becoming the Sea Dogs' all-time leading scorer among defensemen. He was named QMJHL Personality of the Year, QMJHL Defenseman of the Year and Canadian Hockey League Defenseman of the Year.

The Sea Dogs won the 2017 QMJHL championship, and Chabot was awarded playoff MVP after earning 18 assists and 23 points in 18 games and leading all players with a plus-29.

In 2017–18 Chabot bounced between the Senators in Ottawa and Belleville, the American Hockey League affiliate. He played 63 NHL games and had nine goals and 25 points, which tied him for second among NHL rookie defensemen in goals and fifth in points.

Playing with two-time Norris Trophy winner Karlsson accelerated Chabot's development, and he was ready to take over as the team's top rearguard when Karlsson was traded to the San Jose Sharks. Chabot let that be known in the second game of the year with a two-goal, three-point effort against the

L osing all-world defenseman Erik Karlsson in the Ottawa Senators' fire sale was a blow to the team's blue line and fan base, but there was a worthy successor on the roster, waiting just to his left.

Thomas Chabot grew up in Sainte-Marie, Quebec. He spoke only French when he was picked by the Quebec Major Junior Hockey League's Sea Dogs in anglophone Saint John, New Brunswick, but he quickly adapted and became one of the city's favorite sons.

The Senators took him 18th overall in the 2015 draft, and Chabot made his NHL debut in 2016. He played just one game and then watched eight more before being sent back to Saint John for the remainder of the 2016–17 season. Instead of sulking he had 15 points in his first 10 games and then lit the junior

Toronto Maple Leafs, including a dangle and finish worthy of the most offensively gifted forwards.

Chabot had 10 goals and 38 points through the first 38 games of the season, second among NHL defensemen, when he suffered a shoulder injury. A broken toe later in the season also forced him to sit out, but he finished with 41 assists and 55 points in 70 games, putting him 10th among NHL defensemen. Chabot also averaged 24:17 of ice time, just ahead of Norris Trophy winner Mark Giordano, and was fifth in the NHL with 20:45 at even strength.

Days after Karlsson was traded a destructive tornado tore through the Ottawa region. Though incomparable in real-life importance, September 2018 was a rough month in Ottawa and gave the word "rebuild" a new level of gravity as the Sens quickly sank to the bottom of the NHL once the season began.

Chabot was the Senators' lone bright spot, by virtue of his play and personality. He embraced his

anagrammed alter ego Hotsam Batcho, created by Senators superfan Ben Milks, to help sell branded merchandise for the Ottawa Senators Foundation and tornado relief.

"He's a fun-loving guy who always has a smile on his face," said teammate Dylan DeMelo, who came over in the Karlsson trade. "He's really enjoying playing in the NHL. He's living out his dream. You've got to come in and enjoy it every day. He's doing a great job of living in the moment. A lot of guys young and old can learn from that, for sure."

Won silver and named top defenseman and tournament MVP at the 2017 World Junior Championship

Won the QMJHL's Emile "Butch" Bouchard Trophy as best defenseman and named CHL Defenseman of the Year in 2017

Named QMJHL playoff MVP in 2017

Played in the 2019 NHL All-Star Game

RASMUS DAHLIN

ATLANTIC DIVISION | Sabres | Defense

"The greatest ability on the ice is the way he reads the game," said Frolunda coach Roger Ronnberg. "He looks like he's playing in slow-mo. He always has time to make reads and smart plays, and he is getting better in every area."

Mid season, and still just 16, Dahlin played in his first World Juniors, and a year later he truly made a name for himself at the tournament. He was named the top defenseman in 2018, and after a loss to Canada in the gold medal game he was promptly suspended for two games by the International Ice Hockey Federation for taking his silver medal off during the ceremony.

It was part youthful petulance, part competitive passion and something he learned from his idol.

"He's a little like a Peter Forsberg character," according to Team Sweden coach Tomas Monten. "He gets really mean. He has a high temper. That gives him a competitive edge at practices and especially in games. He doesn't lose his head, but he competes."

About six weeks later Dahlin made his Olympic debut for Sweden in PyeongChang, South Korea. At 17 years old he was the team's youngest player by seven years and the first to go from the World Juniors to the Olympics since Hall of Famer Eric Lindros did so with Canada in 1992.

Two-time Norris Trophy winner and fellow Swede Erik Karlsson called Dahlin "much better than I was at that age," and it was preordained that Dahlin would go first overall in the 2018 NHL Entry Draft.

"He is half Karlsson, half [seven-time Norris Trophy winner Nicklas] Lidstrom," said hockey analyst and former NHLer Ray Ferraro. "He defends like Lidstrom and skates like Karlsson. He's more physical than both."

When the Buffalo Sabres surprised no one and chose Dahlin with the team's first number one overall

Rasmus Dahlin is from Lidkoping, Sweden, a town of 25,000 with plenty of hockey. His father, Martin, was a defenseman in Sweden's lower tiers, and his brother, Felix, played professionally until he was forced to retire at 20 because of arthritis. The condition also affects his mother and sister but seems to have skipped Rasmus.

Growing up Dahlin played forward and his favorite player was Peter Forsberg. But when he was 13 it dawned on him that if he played defense he could be on the ice for half the game and dictate the offense from the back.

It was a smart move; just three years later Dahlin joined Frolunda at the top of the Swedish Hockey League for the 2016–17 season.

selection since 1987, he became the first Swede at the top of the draft since Mats Sundin in 1989, and he didn't spend a minute in the minors.

"Rasmus Dahlin is to a franchise what [Connor] McDavid and [Auston] Matthews have meant to the Oilers and Maple Leafs," said television scouting analyst and former NHL general manager Craig Button. "He is to defensemen what those two guys are to centermen. He is a number one, elite defenseman who can play in the NHL right now."

Dahlin played all 82 games and finished second in assists (35) and third in points (44) among all rookies. He was just the third defenseman in NHL history with 40-plus points when starting the season as an 18-year-old, surpassing Bobby Orr's 41 points and second only to the 66 points earned by Phil Housley, his coach until he was dismissed after the Sabres failed to make the playoffs.

"His development has been pretty quick," according to Sabres captain Jack Eichel. "You see some of the stuff he does on the ice and it's just, we in the room laugh about it when he does stuff. And to think he's only 18 years old. He doesn't even know how good he is, to be honest with you. We realize it and we know how good he's going to be, but he's just getting better every day. He's such a good kid and he works hard on the ice. He's got a great attitude. We couldn't be luckier to have him."

Won the European Champions League with Frolunda in 2017

Won silver and named best defenseman at the 2018 World Junior Championship

Named Swedish Junior Player of the Year in 2018, the first 17-year-old to win it since 1984

Selected first overall in the 2018 NHL Entry Draft

Voted a finalist for the Calder Trophy in 2019

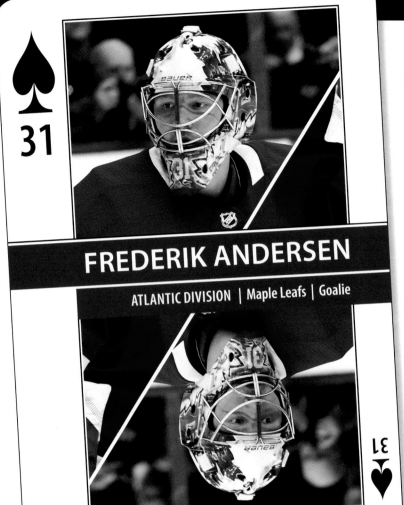

FREDERIK ANDERSEN

ATLANTIC DIVISION | Maple Leafs | Goalie

brothers and cousins.

All three of their children followed in their footsteps; Sebastian played defense in Denmark, Amalie played the same position in a women's league in Sweden and Frederik has made a name for himself in North America.

With stiff competition in Herning, Andersen went to the Frederikshavn White Hawks in 2009 and had a .932 save percentage in 30 games. Then in 2011–12 he crossed the Kattegat to play for legendary Frolunda in the Swedish Hockey League, where he had a 1.62 goals-against average and .943 save percentage, both of which led the league, and he broke Henrik Lundqvist's franchise record with eight shutouts.

After being passed over in two NHL drafts Andersen was taken in the last round in 2010 by the Carolina Hurricanes. He never signed a contract, however, so in 2012 the Anaheim Ducks chose Andersen in the third round, 87th overall. On October 20, 2013, after a year in the American Hockey League, Andersen became the first Danish goalie in NHL history.

In 2014–15 Andersen made his mark on the record books as the fastest goalie in NHL history to reach the 26-win mark (26-5-0), and he tied the record for the fastest to 50 career wins (50-13-5), originally set by Bill Durnan of the Montreal Canadiens in 1944.

The following season Andersen had a 22-9-7 record and shared the William M. Jennings Trophy with partner John Gibson for allowing the fewest goals in the league.

Gibson was the starter of the strongest duo in the league, so the Ducks traded Andersen to the Toronto Maple Leafs in 2016 for a first- and second-round pick. He's since become Toronto's Mr. Consistency.

In his first three seasons with the Leafs Andersen's save percentages were .918, .918, and .917. He's third in the NHL in wins since joining Toronto (107) and

Ernst Andersen was a championship-winning goalie with his hometown Herning Blue Fox in Denmark's top flight, but even as his son Frederik emerged as a star between the pipes he didn't see the NHL in his future.

There wasn't much precedent to go on. Only nine Danes had been drafted before Frans Nielsen, another Herning native, became the first to play in the NHL in 2007. That an Andersen would join him in the world's top league shouldn't have come as much of a surprise, however.

The Andersen family is Danish hockey royalty. Ernst played professionally for 20 years before becoming the national junior team's goalie coach, and his wife, Charlotte, also played, as did a handful of their

he's faced the most shots by a considerable margin — his 6,221 shots against are 550 more than second-place Connor Hellebuyck.

Andersen was first in the NHL with 2,029 saves in 2017–18 and set a Maple Leafs record for wins in a season with 38, good for fourth in the league. In 2018–19 he tied for third in the NHL with 36 wins and was second in saves (1,796) in another season in which his offense-first team left him exposed far too often.

A second straight loss to the Boston Bruins in the playoffs ended a season with great promise, despite Andersen's .922 playoff save percentage, and for the first time he said no to his country. A nagging groin injury needed rest, and after 192 regular-season games played with Toronto, he was tired.

The great Dane had represented his country at the World Championship in 2009, 2010, 2011, 2012 and 2018, at home, when he put on a show at the arena where he watched his dad

and got his start, an arena full of Herning Blue Fox banners and trophies. Denmark fell short of the medals, but Andersen was named the tournament's best goaltender.

Andersen, who turned 30 on the eve of the 2019–20 season, has two years left on his contract. He's the most dependable goalie the Maple Leafs have had in a generation, and for all the offensive glitz assembled in Toronto he will be the key to a long playoff run.

The taciturn Andersen might even crack a smile if he's the first goalie since 1967 to raise the Stanley Cup in a Maple Leafs jersey. He certainly will if he's the first to bring it to Denmark.

Named to the NHL All-Rookie Team in 2013–14
Shared the William M. Jennings Trophy with John Gibson in 2016
Finished first in the NHL in saves in 2017–18 with 2,029
Finished third in the NHL in wins in 2018–19 with 36

METROPOLITAN DIVISION

FIRST TEAM

46	**SIDNEY CROSBY**	Penguins	Center
48	**TAYLOR HALL**	Devils	Left Wing
50	**ALEX OVECHKIN**	Capitals	Left Wing
52	**SETH JONES**	Blue Jackets	Defense
54	**KRIS LETANG**	Penguins	Defense
56	**SERGEI BOBROVSKY**	Blue Jackets	Goalie

SECOND TEAM

58	**NICKLAS BACKSTROM**	Capitals	Center
60	**CLAUDE GIROUX**	Flyers	Center/Left Wing
62	**EVGENI MALKIN**	Penguins	Center
64	**JOHN CARLSON**	Capitals	Defense
66	**ZACH WERENSKI**	Blue Jackets	Defense
68	**BRADEN HOLTBY**	Capitals	Goalie

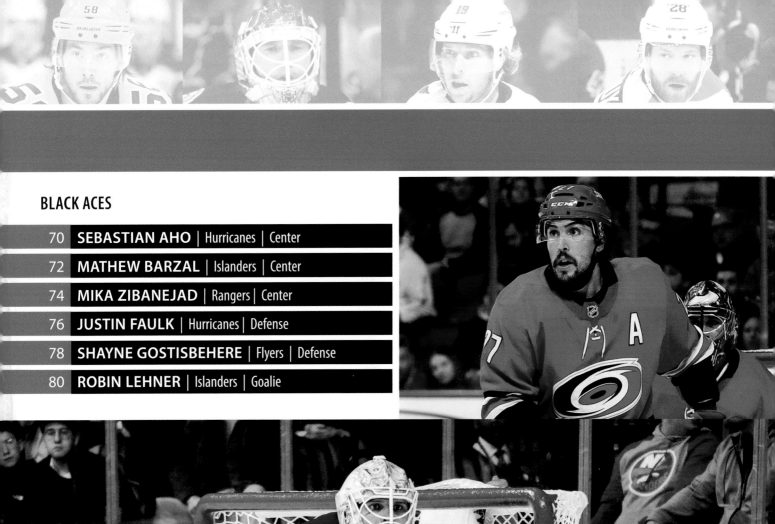

BLACK ACES

70	**SEBASTIAN AHO**	Hurricanes	Center
72	**MATHEW BARZAL**	Islanders	Center
74	**MIKA ZIBANEJAD**	Rangers	Center
76	**JUSTIN FAULK**	Hurricanes	Defense
78	**SHAYNE GOSTISBEHERE**	Flyers	Defense
80	**ROBIN LEHNER**	Islanders	Goalie

SIDNEY CROSBY

Won both the Art Ross Trophy and Hart Trophy in 2007 and 2014

Won the Ted Lindsay Award three times (2007, 2013, 2014)

Won the Stanley Cup three times (2009, 2016, 2017) and the Conn Smythe Trophy twice (2016, 2017)

Won two Olympic golds (2010, 2014)

Won the Maurice Richard Trophy twice (2010, 2017)

The mythology has been established — from the dryer in the family basement to the Great One dubbing him "the Next Big Thing," to the Golden Goal — and the legend only grows.

At the age of 7, Sidney Crosby was "head and shoulders above everyone else his age," according to his hockey camp instructor and future Conn Smythe Trophy winner Brad Richards.

Sid the Kid was 16 when Wayne Gretzky was asked if anyone could break his NHL records. "Yes, Sidney Crosby. He's the best player I've seen since Mario [Lemieux]." Lemieux became Crosby's teammate, mentor, landlord and boss with the Pittsburgh Penguins, who drafted him first overall in 2005 after he led the Canadian Hockey League in scoring and won CHL Player of the Year twice in a row.

Entering the NHL the same year as Alex Ovechkin, Crosby had 102 points — the youngest player in history with over 100 — but lost the 2006 Calder Trophy to Ovechkin, who had 106.

In their sophomore seasons, Crosby topped Ovi with 120 points to win both the 2007 Art Ross and Hart trophies. He was the second-youngest MVP in NHL history, behind Gretzky, and the youngest scoring champion in major professional sports history. Named captain in 2007, the youngest in NHL history at the time, Crosby also became the youngest captain to lift the Stanley Cup in 2009.

With the 2010 Olympics on home soil, Canadians put their hopes on Crosby's 22-year-old shoulders. He had a quiet tournament until the gold medal game when Crosby took a pass from Jarome Iginla and swept it between Ryan Miller's legs at 7:40 of overtime to give Canada a 3–2 victory over the U.S. Crosby has also won gold at the 2005 World Juniors, the 2014 Olympics, the 2015 World Championship and the 2016 World Cup of Hockey.

Through fate and scheduling Sid and Ovi remain tied together. On January 11, 2017, Ovechkin earned his 1,000th NHL point, against the Penguins, naturally. Five days later they played again and

No. 87 — who was born on August 7, 1987 (8/7/87) — had a goal and three assists in an 8–7 win over the Capitals to tie him for 87th on the NHL's all-time scoring list.

A month later Crosby became the 11th youngest player with 1,000 career points, despite missing the equivalent of more than a full season due to serious concussion issues. Reaching it in 757 games he trailed only Gretzky, Lemieux, Bobby Orr and Mike Bossy on the career points-per-game list.

After winning the Stanley Cup in 2016 the Penguins repeated as champions in 2017. They became the first back-to-back winners in the 21st century, the first in the salary cap era and the first playing with a defense corps that hadn't received one Norris Trophy vote in their collective careers. Crosby won his second straight Conn Smythe — the third player in history to do so and first since Lemieux in 1991 and 1992.

In 2018–19 Crosby had his ninth season of 30-plus goals and his sixth 100-point season. It was his first time hitting the century mark since 2013–14, and only Gretzky, Lemieux, Marcel Dionne, Mike Bossy and Peter Stastny have more. It was also the ninth time he finished top 5 in points.

Heading into 2019–20 Crosby was five points up on Ovechkin as the active leader in points (1,216 to 1,211), and despite the Penguins being swept in the first round in 2019 he leads all players in playoff goals (66), assists (120) and points (186) since 2005–06.

Penguins coach Mike Sullivan calls Crosby "the best 200-foot player in the game," but he was overlooked for the Selke, one of the few trophies to elude him, despite being ahead of four-time winner Patrice Bergeron in eight different advanced defensive metrics.

Crosby was named a finalist for the Hart Trophy alongside young guns Connor McDavid and eventual winner Nikita Kucherov.

Sid is no longer a Kid, but he's still at his peak after 14 seasons, and the rest of the NHL's superstars have a long way to go to dethrone the emperor Penguin.

TAYLOR HALL

Kim Strba and Steve Hall were pondering a move back to Ontario from Calgary but couldn't decide where to settle. Kim had family in Toronto, Windsor and Kirkland Lake, Australian-born Steve had grown up in London and they'd met at the University of Guelph.

In the end they chose Kingston. They didn't want to live too close to relatives, so they came up with a "100 mile rule" when relocating.

Steve was a former receiver in the Canadian Football League, and he'd moved his family to Calgary while he was training with the national bobsled team. Their son Taylor, however, was all about hockey. "I had come through this way to play football in Ottawa," said Steve. "I knew [Kingston] was on water and it

was a little farther north, so if you had to build a rink you could. Those things have to be taken into consideration when you have a hockey player."

Taylor Hall was just entering high school when they moved, and the transition wasn't easy. His first season with the Greater Kingston Predators was mediocre as he and his family settled into their new surroundings. But things clicked in his second season with the Predators, who went 27-4 thanks to Hall's 47 goals and 92 points in 32 games.

The Windsor Spitfires took notice and picked Hall second overall in the 2007 Ontario Hockey League draft. He was named Canadian Hockey League Rookie of the Year in 2008, and in 2009 he was named OHL playoff MVP and then tournament

MVP after leading the Spitfires to the Memorial Cup championship.

The following season was dominated by the Taylor/Tyler debate over who would go first overall in the 2010 NHL Entry Draft. Fittingly, Hall and Tyler Seguin tied for the OHL scoring title, but Windsor won its second straight Memorial Cup and Hall became the first player in history to win tournament MVP honors in consecutive seasons.

The rebuilding Edmonton Oilers selected Hall first overall, and he went on to break a couple of Wayne Gretzky's franchise records. On March 30, 2013, Hall recorded the fastest hat trick from the start of a game, scoring three in the first 7:53 to better Gretzky's 12:38 in 1985–86. The second came on October 17, 2013, when Hall scored twice in eight seconds, which topped Gretzky for the quickest two goals in team history by one second.

By the end of 2015–16 Hall had accumulated 328 points in 381 games through six seasons with the Oilers, leading the team in scoring three times and finishing among the NHL's top-10 scorers twice.

The Oilers had been stockpiling offensive talent with high draft picks, including Connor McDavid, and needed help on defense, but it still came as a shock when they made a deal with the Devils.

Edmonton sent Hall to New Jersey in a rare 1-for-1 trade for defenseman Adam Larsson in the summer of 2016, giving then-general manager Peter Chiarelli the distinction of trading both Taylor and Tyler, the latter when he was managing the Boston Bruins.

In his first season in New Jersey Hall had a respectable 53 points in 72 games, but the Devils finished last in the Eastern Conference. Like in midget, however, in year two he broke out and took his team with

him. Hall had a 26-game point streak and finished the 2017–18 season with 39 goals and 93 points. He was sixth in NHL scoring to lead the Devils to the playoffs for the first time since 2012.

Hall was recognized with the Hart Trophy as league MVP, the first winner to be traded at any point in his career since Joe Thornton in 2006.

"If there's one thing I'm proud of, it's to be the first Devil to win MVP," said Hall. "At the start of this season, people wrote us off. People have [written] me off. It feels pretty good standing up here now, and to have the MVP, and to have had a successful season in Jersey."

Hall wouldn't repeat as MVP in 2018–19 after suffering a knee injury and playing only 33 games, albeit with 37 points, but it wasn't all bad luck.

After picking Nico Hershier, Hall's center in his MVP season, first overall in 2017, the Devils won the draft lottery in 2019, which they used to select another center, Jack Hughes. It was the fifth time in his career that Hall's team had gotten the first pick.

Known for his wit, Hall tweeted, "Officially adding 'NHL lottery ball specialist' to my hockey résumé."

Won back-to-back Memorial Cups in 2009 and 2010 and named MVP for both

Taken first overall at the 2010 NHL Entry Draft

Won gold at the 2015 and 2016 World Championship

Selected to three NHL All-Star Games (2016, 2017, 2018)

Awarded the Hart Trophy in 2018

ALEX OVECHKIN

One of hockey's enduring clichés is that it's a game of inches. For Alex Ovechkin the perception of his career almost came down to roughly the width of the shaft on a goalie stick.

Down 1–0 in Game 7 of the second round in the 2017 playoffs, the Washington Capitals captain was alone in the slot for a one-timer that was headed for the top corner and a tie, until the smallest part of Marc-André Fleury's goalie equipment intervened. Maybe the Capitals wouldn't have beaten the Pittsburgh Penguins anyway, but it fed into the narrative that Ovechkin disappears in the biggest games.

Ovechkin was selected first overall in 2004, and Sidney Crosby was the top pick in 2005 by the Penguins. After the 2004–05 lockout they made their NHL debuts in 2005–06, and though they have con-

trasting personalities and styles, they've been compared ever since.

In his first NHL game Ovechkin scored twice and hit an opponent so hard that a partition broke. "Within a week or so we knew that we had a real special human being here," said Glen Hanlon, Ovechkin's first NHL coach.

Later in the season Ovechkin showed the rest of the world. Facing the Phoenix Coyotes on January 16, 2006, Ovechkin was knocked down and sliding on his back as he drove to the net but somehow managed to hook the puck past a stunned Brian Boucher in goal. It was the highlight of the decade, now simply called the Goal, and it's still Ovechkin's favorite.

A decade later, on January 10, 2016, Ovechkin became the fifth-fastest player to reach 500 goals, and a year and a day after that he scored 35 seconds into a game against the Penguins to earn his 1,000th point in his 880th game. He is the fastest active player to reach the milestone.

Crosby reached 1,000 points a month after Ovechkin, and they're one-two in goals and points since 2005–06, when they entered the league. By the end of the 2018–19 season Ovechkin's 658 goals were 212 ahead of Crosby's, and his 1,211 points were just five behind.

Ovechkin beat out Crosby for the 2006 Calder Trophy, but even as he continued to take home individual awards year after year, he once said that he would "trade them all for one Stanley Cup." Yet 12 seasons into his NHL career, Ovechkin still hadn't won hockey's holy grail, while Crosby had won it three times. The Penguins ended Ovi's dream in 2016 and 2017 on their way to consecutive titles, and each of Crosby's three Stanley Cups went through Washington in the second round.

But in 2018 the script was flipped. The Capitals beat the Penguins, in the second round no less, on their way to the first Stanley Cup in franchise history. Ovechkin had 15 goals and 27 points in 24 games to be named the Conn Smythe Trophy winner.

The 6-foot-3, 239-pound Muscovite wrecking ball then took to the streets for a celebration that was historic in scale and social media exposure.

Ovechkin was handed the Cup in Las Vegas after beating the expansion Vegas Golden Knights, and it stayed with him at a nightclub until 5 a.m. Back in Washington he threw out the first pitch at a Washington Nationals game before doing a keg stand with the Cup and taking it for a swim in a fountain in Georgetown. He later brought it to *The Tonight Show*, barbecued and slept with it at his home in Virginia, and showed it a good time around Moscow, including sitting with it to watch the motherland beat Spain at the 2018 World Cup.

There was no hangover, however, at least not in the regular season. The Capitals were eliminated in the first round of the 2019 playoffs, but Ovechkin won his eighth Maurice Richard Trophy after leading the NHL with 51 goals, only the fourth time a player 33 or older had ever scored 50.

If the lockout hadn't shortened the 2012–13 season, when he scored 32 goals in 48 games, it would likely have been Ovechkin's ninth 50-goal season, tying him with Wayne Gretzky and Mike Bossy for the most ever. He's second to Gretzky in goals scored before turning 34 and has an outside shot at breaking his all-time record of 894.

For Ovechkin, arguably the purest and most exciting goal-scorer the game has ever seen, it's a Hall of Fame career. His plaque will be up in the same room as the Stanley Cup that bears his name and still has the faint whiff of alcohol and vindication coming off it.

Won gold at the 2008, 2012 and 2014 World Championship

Won the Hart Trophy three times (2008, 2009, 2013) and the Ted Lindsay Award three times (2008, 2009, 2010)

Won the Art Ross Trophy in 2008

Won the Maurice Richard Trophy eight times (2008, 2009, 2013, 2014, 2015, 2016, 2018, 2019)

Won the Stanley Cup in 2018 and named Conn Smythe Trophy winner

SETH JONES

Won gold at the 2011 and 2012 Under-18 World Championship

Won gold at the 2013 World Junior Championship

Named WHL Rookie of the Year in 2013

Played in two NHL All-Star Games (2017, 2019)

Ronald "Popeye" Jones was a journeyman basketball player, which took him through six NBA cities, including one year in Denver. It was there that his sons fell in love with hockey.

His eldest son, Justin, was the first who wanted to play, but once 6-year-old Seth saw the Colorado Avalanche in Game 7 of the Stanley Cup Final, he was hooked. "They won the Cup there in 2001 and I was able to go to that game," said Seth. "It was Ray Bourque's first Cup and Sakic passed it to him. That jumped up my love for the game . . . You don't get many chances to go to a Stanley Cup game and that was a special one."

Knowing more about the hardwood, Popeye sought advice from Avalanche captain and fellow Pepsi Center tenant Joe Sakic. "He looked and saw how tall I was," recalled Popeye. "Joe wasn't a big guy. He said, 'By the looks of you, they are going to be very tall. Make sure they know how to skate.' I told my boys, 'Joe Sakic said you better know how to skate.'"

So Popeye put his sons into figure skating, and as Seth grew into his 6-foot-4, 210-pound frame he remained a smooth and efficient skater.

If Popeye couldn't impart hockey wisdom on his sons, he could share the lessons he learned through his fascination with the structure of chess. "Control the middle of the ice the way you control the middle of the board and think two or three moves ahead of everyone," advised Popeye.

Seth took to the game quickly, choosing defense because he could see the whole ice and control play strategically. He won his first national title in peewee with the Littleton (Colorado) Hawks.

After two years with the U.S. National Team Development Program, during which he won back-to-back gold medals at the Under-18 World Championship, Jones played for the Western Hockey League's Portland Winterhawks, where he was named WHL Rookie of the Year in 2012–13. He was the number one ranked skater heading into the 2013 NHL Entry Draft, and most experts assumed the

top pick was going to be either Jones or the Halifax Mooseheads' Nathan MacKinnon.

Jones' Team USA won gold at the 2013 World Junior tournament, beating MacKinnon and Canada in the semifinals, but MacKinnon got a small measure of revenge when his Mooseheads beat Jones and the Winterhawks in the 2013 Memorial Cup final.

While a return to Colorado as the first overall selection would have been nice for Jones, the Avalanche took MacKinnon with the top pick. Somewhat surprisingly, Jones fell to the Nashville Predators at fourth.

In Nashville, Jones was stuck behind righties Shea Weber and Ryan Ellis on the depth chart of defensemen, so on January 6, 2016, he was traded to the Columbus Blue Jackets for center Ryan Johansen, a move Jones admitted was devastating.

But the passion of Columbus fans won him over and he grew under the tutelage of coach John Tortorella. In 2017–18 Jones set career highs in goals (16), assists (41) and points (57) and finished fourth in Norris Trophy voting. By the end of 2018–19 he had accumulated 165 points in 269 games over four seasons as a Blue Jacket, and made two All-Star Game appearances.

In 2019 Columbus won a playoff series for the first time in franchise history, but Jones is still chasing the feeling of lifting the Stanley Cup, as he watched Bourque do almost two decades ago and like his idol, Nicklas Lidstrom, did four times.

Lidstrom was 27 when he won his first title and Bourque was 40. The 25-year-old Jones is now entering his prime and already inspiring the next generation, one that looks more like him.

"There have been a few African-American kids who have come up to me and said, 'You're my favorite player,'" said Jones. "I am for whatever I can do to grow the game in all aspects. A black kid cheering for hockey or cheering for me is pretty rare. When you see that, you get pretty excited."

KRIS LETANG

O n the morning of January 29, 2014, Kris Letang woke up dizzy and disoriented. Determined to go on the Pittsburgh Penguins' mother-son road trip, he ignored the symptoms and got on the plane.

Team doctor Dharmesh Vyas didn't let Letang play that night in Los Angeles and arranged for an MRI the next day when the Penguins were in Arizona. Letang, at 26, had suffered a stroke. It was the result of an undiagnosed heart defect that's common in babies but usually repairs itself.

"The whole time, he maintained a really strong perspective on what was going on, but also [remained] extremely optimistic that he was going to continue to play," said Vyas.

That perspective was hard earned, because the specter of an athletic career cut short doesn't compare to what Letang had already endured.

In 2003 the Quebec Major Junior Hockey League's Val-d'Or Foreurs drafted Luc Bourdon third overall and Letang 27th. During the 2004–05 season, Bourdon and Letang each had 13 goals and 19 assists in 70 games, and together they won gold medals with Team Canada at the 2006 and 2007 World Juniors.

Bourdon was drafted 10th overall by the Vancouver Canucks in 2005 while the Penguins took Letang 62nd, and they remained close as their NHL careers took off. After winning the Emile Bouchard Trophy as the QMJHL's Defenseman of the Year in 2007, Letang reached the Stanley Cup Final in his first full season with the Penguins. On May 29, 2008, as Pittsburgh was battling Detroit for the Cup, Bourdon died in a motorcycle crash in New Brunswick at the age of 21.

One year later, after the Penguins defeated the Red Wings in a Stanley Cup rematch, Letang got a tattoo dedicated to his grandmother and Bourdon.

"Every time I step on the ice he's in my thoughts," said Letang. "He was a guy that embraced every day of hockey. Every night I think about him before games, making sure I'm ready and all the things he taught me."

With that inspiration, Letang established himself as a young star and the anchor of the Penguins defense — a smooth-skating, puck-moving defenseman who eats minutes and can be deployed in any situation.

Letang was a Norris Trophy finalist after 38 points in 35 games in the lockout-shortened 2012–13 season, but between 2011 and 2015 he missed 102 games due to ailments, including multiple concussions. When Letang has been healthy he's averaged 0.66 points per game, which is third among defensemen with at least 500 games played since he entered the league.

Back to full strength in 2015–16, Letang averaged almost 27 minutes a game and was third among defensemen with 67 points. In the postseason he averaged just under 29 minutes and had 15 points in 23 games, including the Stanley Cup–winning goal in Game 6 against the San Jose Sharks.

The Penguins repeated as champions in 2017, and despite not playing in the postseason, Letang got his name on the Cup for the third time. He played the minimum 41 regular-season games to be eligible before neck surgery to repair a herniated disc ended his season. During the playoffs he acted as a de facto assistant coach, imparting veteran wisdom and offering inspiration.

If it weren't for bad luck Letang would have no luck at all. In 2018–19 he missed 17 games with knee and neck injuries, the latter aggravated when he came to the defense of partner Brian Dumoulin at an outdoor Stadium Series game. He was still eighth among NHL defensemen with 68 points and fifth in points per game (0.86), the third highest of his distinguished career. He also had his second-highest average ice time, at 25:58 a game, and his 61.6 goals-for percentage at 5-on-5 was third in NHL.

In a rare event in recent NHL history the Penguins were swept out of the playoffs in the first round, which meant that all players were up for trade debate, except maybe the captain.

"I've been there for 13 years and I can't see myself leaving," said the 32-year-old Letang, before adding, "We all know it's a business."

You can't replace the Penguins' all-time leader in goals (112), assists (381) and points (493) by a defenseman, nor a person who donates $58,000 to match his jersey number to pay the medical bills for a 7-year-old leukemia patient who simply asked for a stick. It would be folly to try.

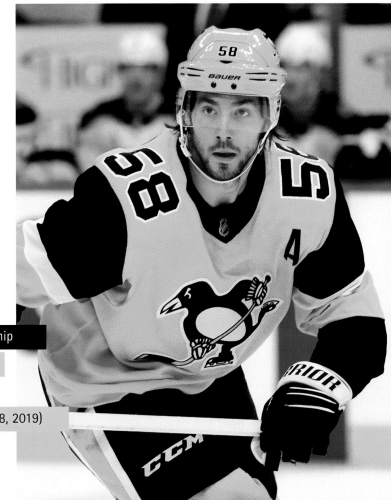

Won gold at the 2006 and 2007 World Junior Championship

Named the QMJHL's Defenseman of the Year in 2007

Won the Stanley Cup three times (2009, 2016, 2017)

Played in five NHL All-Star Games (2011, 2012, 2016, 2018, 2019)

SERGEI BOBROVSKY

SIGNED
Florida Panthers on July 1, 2019

- Won the Vezina Trophy twice (2013, 2017)
- Won gold at the 2014 World Championship
- Played in two NHL All-Star Games (2015, 2017)
- Led the NHL in goals-against average (2.06) and save percentage (.931) in 2016–17
- Led the NHL in shutouts in 2018–19 with nine

As an undrafted free agent Sergei Bobrovsky rose from obscurity to become a Vezina Trophy winner in 2013. But by 2015–16 Bobrovsky had fallen on hard times, plagued by groin injuries that robbed him of his swagger.

Bobrovsky is a gym rat, not always a common trait among the goalie fraternity, but the extra weight that he carried in muscle was working against him. So prior to the 2016–17 season he dropped about 15 pounds.

"You look at his body last year and the body composition, and all his body fats and all that, you'd say it was impossible," said Blue Jackets general manager Jarmo Kekalainen. "But he did it . . . That just tells you about his dedication and how serious he is about his professionalism and how he approaches every day."

Having grown up in Siberia, Bobrovsky comes by his work ethic honestly. His father was a coal miner, and his mother worked on the line at a steel factory.

Bobrovsky spent three seasons with his hometown Metallurg Novokuznetsk in the Kontinental Hockey League before the Philadelphia Flyers offered him a contract in 2010. He made his NHL debut in Philly's first game of 2010–11, becoming the youngest goalie in Flyers history to start a season. But the city and franchise have a way of chewing up and spitting out goaltenders and Bobrovsky lasted only two years before being traded to the Blue Jackets in 2012.

It paid immediate dividends in Ohio. Bobrovsky won the Vezina in the lockout-shortened 2012–13 season and finished fifth in Hart Trophy voting.

In 2014 Bobrovsky returned home to represent Russia at the Sochi Olympics, a disappointing showing for the host country. There was, however, redemption for Russia at the 2014 World Championship, as Bobrovsky finished tops in both goals-against average (1.13) and save percentage (.950) to lead the team to gold.

The following two seasons weren't as kind to Bobrovsky. The low point was the 2.75 goals-against average and .908 save percentage in only 37 games played in 2015–16 as he battled his groin injuries.

But newly lean and flexible after revamping his off-season training regimen, Bobrovsky shut out Finland to send Russia to the semifinals of the 2016 World Cup of Hockey. He stopped 91 of 96 shots in the tournament and stood on his head in the semis against eventual champion Canada, with 42 saves.

"Bob" had been put back together again, in mind and body, and his 2.06 goals-against average and .931 save percentage in 2016–17 both led the NHL. He had a career-high 41 wins and won the Vezina for the second time, and the Blue Jackets were the NHL's biggest surprise, finishing fourth overall, up from 27th the year before.

By 2018–19 Bobrovsky was in the final year of his contract and was set to leave Columbus as an unrestricted free agent at season's end. As the trade deadline approached, the Blue Jackets were barely on the playoff bubble, but Kekalainen bet on his own team and resisted the urge to deal his star goalie. Bobrovsky rewarded his faith in him by going 11-5 down the stretch to help Columbus to a wild-card berth. He finished the season first in the NHL in shutouts (nine) and second in wins (37).

Heading into the 2019 postseason Bobrovsky had had a middling playoff history, but he gave Columbus a farewell gift and increased his own stock with the first series victory in franchise history. He allowed just eight goals in a first-round sweep of the dominant Tampa Bay Lightning.

Holding his team in its second-round series against the Boston Bruins, chants of "Bob, Bob, Bob" reverberated around Nationwide Arena. "You hear it," said Bobrovsky. "The fan support in our building is unreal. It's so much fun to play in front of them."

But after seven seasons in a Blue Jackets jersey — during which he was tied for second in the NHL in save percentage (.921), tied for third in wins (213) and tied for seventh in goals-against average (2.40) — Bobrovsky took his talents to South Beach, or just north of there, to play for the Florida Panthers.

The simplest of chants was also a goodbye.

NICKLAS BACKSTROM

METROPOLITAN DIVISION

Capitals | Center | 19

If you research Nicklas Backstrom's accomplishments you might think he played in the 2009 NHL All-Star Game. He didn't, that was Niklas (not Nicklas), the Finnish goalie who spent 10 years in the NHL. And don't confuse him with the other Niklas Backstrom, who is Swedish like Nicklas but a mixed martial arts fighter.

It's typical of the hockey-playing Swedish Backstrom to be lost in the shuffle, and frankly he doesn't care. "Nick's not that person that seeks attention or wants to be that way," said recently retired Henrik Zetterberg, who played with Backstrom on Team Sweden. "He doesn't want to stand out."

It's fitting, then, that Alex Ovechkin took the stage at the 2006 NHL Entry Draft to announce the Washington Capitals had selected Backstrom fourth overall. While Backstrom would be at center and Ovechkin on the wing, there's a strong gravitational pull around Ovi — everything orbits around him in Washington.

Backstrom spent the season after the draft playing for Brynas IF in his hometown of Gavle, the same team his father was on for 10 seasons. He was named the Swedish Hockey League's Rookie of the Year in 2006, and he became the youngest player to represent Sweden at the 2006 World Championship, where he won gold.

In 2007–08, his first season with the Capitals, Backstrom set a franchise rookie record with 55 assists. He was the first rookie in NHL history with consecutive games of at least four assists and finished second to Patrick Kane in Calder Trophy voting. In the playoffs he scored in four straight games in a first-round loss, a sign of things to come.

Backstrom, who led the NHL in assists with 60 in

2014–15, has since become the first player in franchise history with 500 career assists. The milestone came on January 7, 2017, and four days later Backstrom set up Ovechkin for the Russian sniper's 1,000th career point. Over the decade they've played together, Backstrom has assisted on roughly 45 percent of Ovechkin's goals.

No player has more assists than Backstrom's 642 since he entered the league, and just four players have more points. Yet somehow he wasn't named to his first All-Star Game until 2016, his ninth season.

"It's funny," said Barry Trotz, Backstrom's coach at the time. "He's going, 'I've never been. What should I expect?' I'm looking at him, and I'm going, 'You should have been there like 10 times already.'"

When asked about the lack of recognition, Backstrom said, "I don't really care about that stuff. There's a little bit of Swedish culture, I think, to put your team in front of yourself."

It's a positive attitude to have, and it helped the Capitals rid themselves of an albatross with the first Stanley Cup in franchise history. Backstrom had 18 assists and 23 points in 20 postseason games in 2018, while playing with two fractures in his hand that he suffered in the second round against the Pittsburgh Penguins, the team's greatest playoff nemesis.

"Everybody knows that Nicky is maybe the best passer in the league," said teammate Lars Eller. "His hands are very important to him, and they weren't at 100 percent functionality. So for him to go out and play as well as he did, that was special and really speaks to his character."

After scoring 22 goals and 52 assists during the 2018–19 regular season, Backstrom led the Capitals with five goals and had eight points in a seven-game first-round loss to the Carolina Hurricanes. His 106 career playoff points are seventh in the NHL since his first season, and his 70 assists are tied for sixth with Jonathan Toews, winner of three Stanley Cups and a Conn Smythe Trophy.

Like Toews, Backstrom is a playmaker with a strong defensive game. Unlike the Blackhawks captain, Backstrom hasn't received Selke Trophy recognition. "Not enough people talk about him, it's crazy to me," said Capitals analyst and former NHLer Alan May.

Trotz coached Backstrom for four years in Washington and knew what he had in the team's number one center. "When he's said and done and you probably look at his numbers, you're going to go, 'Those might be the quietest Hall of Fame numbers that we've ever seen.'"

No need to wait that long to appreciate the understated and largely anonymous superstar. By the end of 2018–19 Backstrom had 873 points in 895 games, and he's still in his prime. If he plays until his late 30s he could well scale the Mount Rushmore of Swedish forwards — the Sedins, Daniel Alfredsson and Mats Sundin — on his way to the scoring summit.

And there's no hiding there.

Named the Swedish Hockey League's Rookie of the Year in 2006

Won gold at the 2006 and 2017 World Championship

Won silver at the 2014 Olympics

Played in the 2016 NHL All-Star Game

Won the Stanley Cup in 2018

CLAUDE GIROUX

Won gold at the 2008 World Junior Championship

Named QMJHL Playoff MVP in 2008

Played in six NHL All-Star Games (2011, 2012, 2015, 2016, 2018, 2019)

Won gold at the 2015 World Championship

Won the World Cup of Hockey in 2016

It was an inauspicious start. When called upon to select the 22nd pick of the 2006 NHL Entry Draft, then-Philadelphia Flyers general manager and former captain Bobby Clarke approached the podium and promptly forgot the name of the player he wanted. It's a good thing he remembered because he was drafting a future star and captain in Claude Giroux.

The undersized center from Hearst, Ontario, was used to being overlooked, having been passed over by every Ontario Hockey League team in his draft year. Undeterred, Giroux walked on with the Gatineau Olympiques of the Quebec Major Junior Hockey League when he was 15. "My dream was to play in the NHL," recalled Giroux, "but I didn't think I had a chance."

His odds improved greatly when he scored 103 points in the 2005–06 season, and after being drafted he returned to Gatineau and upped his total to 112 points in 2006–07.

The following year Giroux helped Canada win gold at the World Juniors, and he capped the season with the Guy Lafleur Trophy as playoff MVP after leading Gatineau to the 2008 QMJHL title.

In 2009–10, his first full year in the NHL, Giroux played in all 82 NHL games and scored the deciding shootout goal in the season finale against the New York Rangers to send the Flyers to the playoffs.

They carried that momentum all the way to the Stanley Cup Final, losing to the Chicago Blackhawks in six games. Giroux had 10 goals and 21 points in 23 playoff games, including the overtime winner in Game 3 of the final.

If that magical spring didn't launch Giroux to the top, the following seasons did. In 2011–12 Giroux set a career high with 93 points. Then in Game 2 of the second round he set a franchise single-game playoff record with six points, including a hat trick, against the cross-state rival Pittsburgh Penguins.

After the Flyers traded Mike Richards and Jeff Carter the door was then open for Giroux to take a leadership role. On January 15, 2013, he was named

the 19th captain in franchise history.

Philadelphia is a notoriously tough sports town, and the DNA of the Broad Street Bullies remains in the Flyers. Giroux was not created in the image of Clarke or Eric Lindros or Chris Pronger. At 5-foot-11 and 185 pounds, he leads by positive example, silky skill instead of brute strength. He's a playmaker, with smarts, creativity and joie de vivre.

In 2013–14 Giroux finished third in the NHL with 86 points and in Hart Trophy voting. His production then dropped all the way down to 58 by 2016–17, but after a move to left wing the following season he set new career highs in goals (34), assists (68) and points (102). He finished second to Connor McDavid in scoring and was fourth in line for the Hart. It was a 44-point improvement on the season prior, and his plus-minus rating increased by 43 — a major reversal after three years of decline, partly a result of hip and abdominal surgery in 2016.

Turning 31 during the 2018–19 season Giroux continued to buck the aging trend with 85 points, the fourth highest of his career, and played all 82 games for the third season in a row. Despite the career renaissance the Flyers missed the playoffs and haven't won a round since 2012.

The highlight of Giroux's season might have been when the Olympiques retired his number. Former coach Benoit Groulx called him the best player he ever had. "Not only the best, but for me the way he would score goals, the passion, the grit, the way he did it, it's never seen from me at that level," said Groulx. "He was scoring goals, he was the most-liked player on our team. He would score goal after goal for our team, and always a team-first guy."

That's not the only place Giroux left a lasting impression. The graduate of the Hearst Lumber Kings is also in the hearts and logo of his hometown. Giroux helped fund the Hearst Lumberjacks, and when each player pulls on the jersey with a crest that features Giroux's initials and number, they'll remember the kid from their remote town who wasn't drafted in major junior but is now one of the NHL's brightest stars.

EVGENI MALKIN

At the 2017 All-Star weekend, the NHL named its top 100 players from its first 100 years. There were six active players on the list. Evgeni Malkin wasn't one of them.

These types of lists are hotly debated, but Geno was a glaring omission. There are few NHL players more decorated than Malkin, but one happens to be on his team, and that might explain the snub.

Malkin was born in Magnitogorsk, Russia, an iron and steel town on the Ural River. The resources gave the Metallurg hockey team its name, and he joined its system when he was 5 years old. At 17 Malkin was signed to Metallurg's senior team for the 2003–04 season. At the end of the year he was one of the greatest consolation prizes in NHL draft history, going second overall to the Pittsburgh Penguins, after the Washington Capitals took Alex Ovechkin.

Malkin played two more years in Magnitogorsk and had signed the richest contract in the Russian Super League, but he longed to be in the U.S. Malkin left the team during training camp in Helsinki and hid out until he could get his American visa. "This is pure sports terrorism," said Metallurg general manager Gennady Velichkin, who tried to sue the Penguins.

Sidney Crosby had already arrived in Pittsburgh as the top pick in 2005, and it soon became apparent that the Penguins had the 21st century version of Mario Lemieux and Jaromir Jagr.

Malkin made his Penguins debut in 2006–07 and didn't disappoint. He set a modern-day record by scoring in each of his first six games. The only other player to do that was Joe Malone of the Montreal Canadiens in 1917–18. Malkin finished the year with 33 goals, 85 points and the Calder Trophy.

The Penguins lost the 2008 Stanley Cup Final to the Detroit Red Wings, after Malkin had 106 regular-season points. A year later he led the league in scoring with 113 points, and the Penguins beat Detroit in a rematch to win the Cup. With 14 goals and 36 points in 24 games, Malkin became the second-youngest player in history to win the Conn Smythe Trophy.

Over his first four seasons Malkin was one of only three players to average more than a point a game each year, Crosby and Ovechkin being the other two. In 2011 he was averaging just under a point a game when he tore his ACL and MCL, ending his season.

Malkin returned in 2011–12 with a chip on his shoulder and the team on his back. With Crosby suffering from post-concussion syndrome, Malkin had a career-high 50 goals and 109 points to win his second Art Ross. He also won the Hart Trophy and the Ted Lindsay Award.

"With Sid out, teams are paying more attention to him," said teammate Kris Letang. "They're playing him harder. And he likes that."

At 6-foot-3 and 195 pounds, Malkin can do it with power and finesse, a rare combination that's reminiscent of Lemieux. "In sheer skill level Geno probably has to be rated higher [than Crosby]," said former Pittsburgh coach Dan Bylsma. "There's magic there, a little bit different than what Sid has."

Together Malkin and Crosby won their second Stanley Cup in 2016 and then went past Lemieux and Jagr with a third in 2017. Malkin led all scorers with 28 points in the playoffs that season.

While the Penguins celebrated, general manager Jim Rutherford mused about the 100 Greatest Players list of a few months earlier. "Maybe we can revote and see if Malkin is in the top 100 now."

Malkin further built his case with a 98-point season in 2017–18. A rib injury slowed him in 2018–19 and limited him to 68 games, but he still had 72 points and broke the 1,000 career points barrier. He's now third in points since he made his NHL debut (1,002), behind Crosby and Ovechkin, and he trails only Crosby in points per game (1.29 to 1.18).

With a teammate and a compatriot who tend to suck all the oxygen out of the best active player conversation, Malkin is chronically underappreciated. But looking at the list of people behind him on the points-per-game list puts it in historical perspective. It includes Jean Beliveau, Gordie Howe, Bobby Hull, Mark Messier and Steve Yzerman, and the 16 players immediately following him are either in the Hall of Fame or will be near-unanimous choices.

It's Malkin's destiny too, and at the Hall there are no rankings, just respect.

Won the Calder Trophy in 2007

Won the Stanley Cup three times (2009, 2016, 2017)

Won the Conn Smythe Trophy in 2009

Won the Art Ross Trophy twice (2009, 2012)

Won the Hart Trophy and Ted Lindsay Award in 2012

JOHN CARLSON

Won the Calder Cup in 2009 and 2010

Won gold at the 2010 World Junior Championship, scoring the overtime winner

Won the Stanley Cup in 2018

Played in the 2019 NHL All-Star Game and won the hardest shot competition

Leading the NHL in any offensive category generally leads to trophy recognition, but not if you're John Carlson, and that's okay with him.

After being first in defensive scoring in 2017–18 Carlson finished a distant fifth in Norris Trophy voting. He was five points ahead of winner Victor Hedman but 91 first-place votes adrift.

Granted, there's far more to defense than points, but Carlson is as complete as they come. "He doesn't have the flash and flair that some of these other guys have," said teammate T.J. Oshie. "They're going up the ice, toe-dragging guys and all this stuff, but to me he seems impossible to get by as a defenseman. He plays in all situations, and he led the NHL in points by a defenseman, so people are leaving him out, but I don't think he's too upset by it. He's very team-oriented, and you see that in his play."

Born in Natick, Massachusetts, and raised in Colonia, New Jersey, Carlson idolized the New Jersey Devils' Scott Stevens while playing for the New Jersey Rockets. He graduated from there to the Indiana Ice of the United States Hockey League at the age of 17 and was drafted 27th overall by the Capitals in 2008.

Carlson then chose to play for the Ontario Hockey League's London Knights and in his one season in London he was named the Knights' MVP. He had 76 points (16 goals, 60 assists) in 59 games and 22 more (seven goals, 15 assists) in 14 postseason games.

After the Knights were eliminated in the third round, Carlson joined the Hershey Bears for the American Hockey League playoffs and helped them win the 2009 Calder Cup.

Carlson had a brief NHL cameo early in 2009–10 before being sent back down to the minors and joining Team USA for the 2010 World Juniors. He scored the golden goal in overtime against Canada in the championship game, earning the U.S. its first gold since 2004. It was his second goal of the game and he was named to the all-tournament team.

Back with the Capitals late in the season, Carlson scored his first NHL goal on March 25, 2010, and

his first playoff goal in Game 2 of a first-round loss to the Montreal Canadiens. After the Capitals bowed out he joined Hershey for the AHL playoffs and added to his clutch credentials by scoring the goal that won the Bears their second straight Calder Cup.

In the NHL to stay by 2010–11 Carlson was named to the All-Rookie Team and came fifth in Calder Trophy voting after earning 37 points. Since then he is tied for seventh among all NHL defensemen in assists (308) and ranks eighth in points (397).

After finishing the 2017–18 season with career highs in goals (15), assists (53) and points (68), Carlson took it to another level in the playoffs, again leading all defensemen in points with 20 (five goals, 15 assists) and a plus-11 rating in 24 games as the Capitals won the franchise's first Stanley Cup after years of disappointment.

"Last year, he got robbed for the Norris, I think," said teammate Nicklas Backstrom. "If you look around the league and look at all the defensemen, I mean, John Carlson is the guy that I would pick first."

The organization knew what they had in the 6-foot-3, 218-pound defenseman and signed Carlson to an eight-year, $64 million contract just before he hit the free agent market.

Far from being complacent with the money, in 2018–19 Carlson upped his career highs in assists (57) as well as points (70), which were fourth among NHL defensemen, while averaging a new career high in ice time at 25:04. He also went to his first All-Star Game and won the hardest shot competition with a 102.8-mile-per-hour slap shot, topping Alex Ovechkin's 101.3-mile-per-hour winner from the year prior for bragging rights.

Carlson still wasn't a finalist for the 2019 Norris Trophy, but he has a new contract and a Colonial mansion in the D.C. suburbs, where he lives with his family. He also has a Stanley Cup ring — the only thing that really matters to hockey players.

As Carlson said, "At the end of the day, I got what I wanted."

ZACH WERENSKI

Zach Werenski was determined to enter college a year early so he completed his entire senior year of high school in one summer. The native of Grosse Pointe, Michigan, had already started at the University of Michigan when he returned home to write one last exam.

At 17 Werenski was the youngest player in the NCAA, yet he was already 6-foot-2 and over 200 pounds as a freshman. He led the Wolverines defense in scoring and the conference in goals among defensemen and was named to the All-Big Ten first team as well as the Big Ten All-Freshman team. "He looked like a senior, just the way he was built," said Maple Leaf Zach Hyman of his former Michigan teammate.

It wasn't just his size that impressed. The Werenskis were devoted Detroit Red Wings fans, and Zach grew up admiring Nicklas Lidstrom, particularly his calmness with the puck, which he brought to his own game.

The Columbus Blue Jackets liked his combination of size and serenity and drafted Werenski eighth overall in 2015.

Returning to Michigan for his sophomore season, he ranked second in scoring among all NCAA defenders and captained the bronze medal–winning Team USA at the 2016 World Juniors. He led all defensemen with nine points and all skaters with a plus-10 rating en route to being named the best defenseman.

Forgoing his last two years of college, Werenski got his first taste of professional hockey toward the end of the 2015–16 American Hockey League season. He joined the Lake Erie Monsters for the last seven games of the regular season and the playoffs. Werenski had nine assists and 14 points in 17 postseason games as the Monsters won the Calder Cup. He ranked second among AHL defensemen in playoff scoring, with the most assists and points by an 18-year-old in AHL playoff history.

There was nothing left for Werenski to conquer but the NHL, and in 2016–17 the rookie had 47 points in 78 games, with a plus-17 rating and only 14 penalty minutes.

The second-youngest defenseman in the NHL, Werenski was the top scorer among rookie blue-liners, was seventh in overall rookie scoring and had the sixth-most points by a rookie teenage defenseman in NHL history. He set a Blue Jackets record for points by a rookie, which was also the second-most points by a defenseman in franchise history. Werenski averaged almost 21 minutes per game and had the best possession rating of all Blue Jackets defensemen. He helped the team to a 16-game winning streak, one shy of the NHL record, and a 50-win, 108-point season.

The 2016–17 season ended a little more painfully, however. In the third game of the playoffs against the Pittsburgh Penguins, a Phil Kessel shot rode up his stick and hit Werenski in the face, leading to a right eye that was 50 shades of black and swollen shut.

After trying to play with a full visor, Werenski was taken out of the game and declared finished for the season, which ended two games later when Columbus was eliminated. "Balls as big as the building," is how Blue Jackets coach John Tortorella described Werenski's effort to return to the game.

Werenski was a finalist for the Calder Trophy, behind Auston Matthews and Patrik Laine, so his first year isn't remembered just for the size of his black eye or anything else on his anatomy.

By the end of 2018–19 Werenski had accumulated 128 points (38 goals and 90 assists) in 237 games over three seasons in Columbus. His rookie year remains his high-water mark in points, but his ice time, 5-on-5 points and primary assists have all risen each season, and he has reached the playoffs every year. The high point in the 2019 postseason came when the team swept the Presidents' Trophy–winning Tampa Bay Lightning in the first round for the first series win in franchise history.

After falling to the Boston Bruins in the second round, the Blue Jackets lost franchise pillars in Sergei Bobrovsky, Artemi Panarin and Matt Duchene to free agency during the off-season, but Werenski remains part of the foundation, along with fellow blue-chip blue-liner Seth Jones. Still just 22, Werenski is gaining experience with every year — strengthening his defense and giving coaches the confidence to put him out to kill penalties and protect leads.

All that's left for the young leader is to grow a decent playoff beard.

Won bronze at the 2016 World Junior Championship and named best defenseman

Named a First Team All-American and Big Ten Defensive Player of the Year in 2016

Voted a finalist for the Calder Trophy in 2017

Set the Blue Jackets record for points by a rookie

Played in the 2018 NHL All-Star Game

BRADEN HOLTBY

Goaltenders are generally known to be weird, with their quirks and superstitions bred in the solitude of the crease. However, among the eccentrics of the goalie fraternity, Braden Holtby seems odd in his normalcy. But still waters run deep. "He's a competitive freak," according to former Capitals teammate Michael Latta. "Then off the ice he's such a nice, relaxed guy. Chill, really into music and really cool."

Braden's hockey genes came from his father, Greg, who was a goalie with the Western Hockey League's Saskatoon Blades; the music came from his mother, Tami, who was the winner of the Saskatchewan Female Vocalist of the Year award in 1996.

In Lloydminster, Saskatchewan, the Holtby farm often doubled as a rehearsal space. After practic-ing, Tami's bandmates would take shots on Braden, because that's all he ever wanted to do.

Having exhausted his supply of goalie knowledge when his son was 15, Greg hired goalie coach and sports psychologist John Stevenson. Braden was talent-ed but prone to temper tantrums, so Stevenson's grasp of the mental game was a helpful bonus.

In 2006 Braden went to Saskatoon to backstop the Blades. In his first two seasons as a starter Holtby had a mediocre 42-58-11 record, and he didn't get selected until the fourth round of the 2008 NHL Entry Draft, when the Washington Capitals chose him 93rd over-all. Buoyed by their belief in him, he had a 40-16-4 record in 2008–09 and led the Blades to the playoffs for the first time in three years.

Holtby spent three seasons with the American Hockey League's Hershey Bears, where he earned the nickname Holtbeast, before he got a real shot with the Capitals. He proved he belonged in the 2012 playoffs, with a 1.95 goals-against average and .935 save percentage in 14 games, which included a first-round win over the defending champion Boston Bruins.

In 2013–14, Holtby, still fighting for the number one job, was struggling, so Stevenson was called in to help. His training included white pucks and a machine called the CogniSens NeuroTracker to hone mental processing and peripheral vision. He also taught Holtby how to refocus during games, leading to his habit of squirting water after giving up a goal and watching one droplet hit the ice.

In 2014–15 Holtby led the NHL in games played (73) and finished second in wins (41). He had nine shutouts, tied for the most in team history, and twice broke the franchise record for consecutive games played. The following season his 48 wins tied Martin Brodeur's single-season record, in 12 fewer games. He also had a 2.20 goals-against average and .922 save percentage to win the 2016 Vezina Trophy.

In 2016–17, Holtby won the William M. Jennings Trophy and was a finalist for the Vezina again. His 42 wins tied for the league lead, he was first with nine shutouts and his goals-against average (2.07) and save percentage (.925) were both an improvement on the previous year.

For the third straight season, however, the Capitals bowed out in the second round, and a year later Holtby had lost the starter's job to Philipp Grubauer after struggling late in the 2017–18 regular season.

But after Grubauer lost Washington's first two playoff games, Holtby was given another chance, and he quickly returned to form. He helped the Capitals to series wins over Columbus and Pittsburgh and had consecutive shutouts in Games 6 and 7 of the Eastern Conference Final against Tampa Bay. Then in Game 2 of the Stanley Cup Final against the Vegas Golden Knights Holtby's miraculous late-game save on Alex Tuch turned the tide of the series as he backstopped the Capitals to the franchise's first Stanley Cup. He posted a .922 save percentage and 2.16 goals-against average and finished third in Conn Smythe Trophy voting.

Holtby finished the 2018–19 season with a 2.82 goals-against average and a .911 save percentage. His 32 wins made him just the 12th goalie in NHL history to have five straight seasons with 30 or more wins.

While the Capitals lost in seven games in the first round, Holtby's numbers improved in the postseason, as they tend to do. He now sports a career 2.09 goals-against average and .928 save percentage in the playoffs, both tops in the NHL since he entered the league, and he's tied with Corey Crawford for most wins with 48. Those are the numbers of a (Holt)beast.

Tied the single-season record for wins in 2015–16 (48)

Won the World Cup of Hockey in 2016

Played in four NHL All-Star Games (2016, 2017, 2018, 2019)

Won the Vezina Trophy in 2016 and the William M. Jennings Trophy twice (2016, 2017)

Won the Stanley Cup in 2018

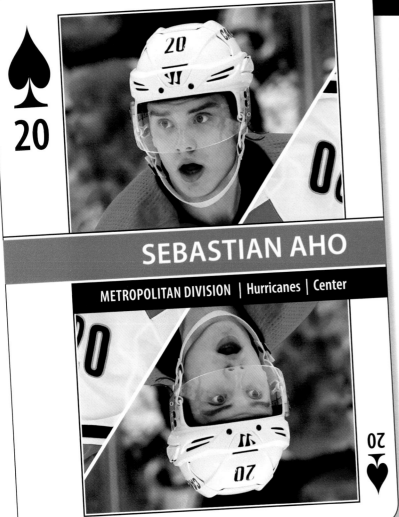

SEBASTIAN AHO

METROPOLITAN DIVISION | Hurricanes | Center

There are two Sebastian Ahos, and not in a metaphysical warrior on the ice, gentleman off the ice kind of way. There are literally two — Sebastian Johannes Aho, a defenseman from Umea, Sweden, on the western side of the Gulf of Bothnia, who played 22 games for the New York Islanders in 2017–18, and Sebastian Antero Aho, a Carolina Hurricanes forward from Rauma, Finland, on the eastern side of the gulf, who played in his first All-Star Game in 2019. This is about the latter.

The Finnish Aho was chosen by the Hurricanes in the second round, 35th overall, of the 2015 NHL draft as he watched on his laptop in Helsinki. Swedish Aho was eligible but wasn't drafted until 2017.

"We saw this kid and loved him," said then-Hurricanes general manager Ron Francis. "I just wanted to make sure we got the forward. That's the one we wanted."

After being drafted by Carolina, Aho spent another season with Finland's Oulun Karpat, where his father, Harri, played and now works as sports director. "It was my dream to play for Karpat my whole childhood. When I got to play for them, it was huge," said Aho.

Aho had 45 points in 45 games in the Liiga in 2015–16, and over the holidays he played on a line with 2016 draft studs Patrik Laine and Jesse Puljujarvi at the World Juniors. The host Finns beat Canada and Sweden before topping Russia for gold, and the linemates were the three top scorers in the tournament. Aho's 14 points in seven games were sandwiched between them, just as he was as the center and defensive conscience of the line.

There's a steep learning curve at center in the NHL and Aho started on the wing. He had 49 points in his rookie year, which climbed to 65 in 2017–18 despite his sitting out for four games with a concussion, the only time he's missed in his career.

At season's end he shone on the international stage once again. Aho had nine goals and 18 points and was plus-15 in eight games at the 2018 World Championship. He was second in tournament scoring behind Patrick Kane and first in points per game at 2.25. Although Finland lost in the quarterfinals he was named the tournament's best forward.

When former Hurricane Rod Brind'Amour took over as head coach in 2018–19 he was initially reluctant to move Aho to center. But the veteran of over 1,600 NHL regular and postseason games knew his young star was ready for the added responsibility. "I think he could play defense, if he had to," said Brind'Amour. "He's a very smart hockey player."

Aho began the season with a 12-game point streak

that included at least one assist in each game, both of which set franchise records and matched Wayne Gretzky (1982–83) and Ken Linseman (1985–86) as the only players to have an assist in the first 12 games to start a season. Aho finished with a team-leading 30 goals and 83 points in 82 games and was the Hurricanes' All-Star Game representative.

A torrid second half earned the Hurricanes a wild-card playoff berth, their first since 2009. The "bunch of jerks," as broadcaster Don Cherry called them in reference to their choreographed and charming victory celebrations, surprised the hockey world by upsetting the defending Stanley Cup champion Washington Capitals in seven games and then sweeping the Islanders. Aho led the team again in the postseason with 12 points in 15 games.

In a league where Nicklas Backstrom once scored on Niklas Backstrom, the Vancouver Canucks had two players named Greg Adams, and the Hurricanes'

Justin Faulk is in the same conference as Justin Falk of the Ottawa Senators, the 22-year-old Aho has really made a name for himself.

The restricted free agent also inspired the first offer sheet the NHL has seen in six years, by the Montreal Canadiens. The Hurricanes quickly matched it to keep their most talented player and future leader.

"There's no doubt in my mind that one day he'll be the captain of the team," predicted general manager Don Waddell. "There's no selfishness in his game. I can't say enough good things about him."

Won gold at the 2016 World Junior Championship

Named best forward at the 2018 World Championship

Set franchise records in 2018–19 with a 12-game point streak that included at least one assist in each game to start the season

Played in the 2019 NHL All-Star Game

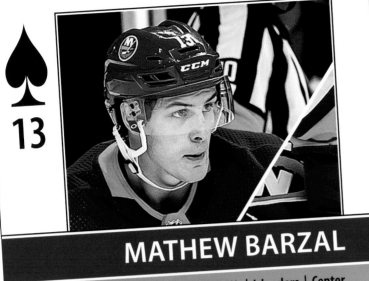

MATHEW BARZAL

METROPOLITAN DIVISION | Islanders | Center

Columbia, native and product of the Burnaby Winter Club first in the 2012 bantam draft.

Instead of sulking Barzal went on to become the WHL's Western Conference Player of the Year after finishing with 10 goals and 79 points in only 41 games. He followed that up by leading Seattle to its first WHL championship and being named the 2017 playoff MVP, with 25 points (seven goals and 18 assists) in 16 games.

"It sucked at the start, but you get over it and just focus on being a more complete player," said Barzal. "If you let that stuff hold you back — or if you develop a bit-terness toward people — it just takes away from your game, and you have to make the best of it."

As an alternate captain for Team Canada, Barzal also had eight points in seven games at the 2017 World Juniors and won silver.

And what a difference a year makes. Barzal stuck with the Islanders the follow-ing season and became the first rookie in franchise history to have five assists in one game, in a 6–4 win against the Colorado Avalanche on November 5, 2017.

Barzal finished 2017–18 with 22 goals and led the Islanders with 85 points. His 63 assists tied a franchise record and was the third-highest total by a rookie in NHL history. He was also just the fourth rookie in the salary cap era to average more than a point a game while playing more than half the season, joining Alex Ovechkin, Evgeni Malkin, Connor McDavid, and his idol, Sidney Crosby. Only Barzal, Crosby, Ovechkin and Malkin had at least 85 points.

It made the Calder Trophy voting nearly unanimous. Barzal received 160 first-place votes to just two for second-place Brock Boeser of the Vancouver Canucks.

"Barzal is a good two-way guy and probably one of the best skaters in the NHL already," assessed Boeser, who first faced Barzal at a bantam tournament in

Mathew Barzal's first NHL game wasn't exactly the stuff of childhood dreams. Chosen 16th overall in the 2015 NHL Entry Draft by the New York Islanders, after they traded up to get him, he was in the lineup on opening night of the 2016–17 season. His box score included three penalties, two in the first 5:06 of the game, four lost faceoffs of six taken, and no shots on net.

"I'd played exhibition games and I'd been through training camp, but there's nothing like playing in a regular-season NHL game," understated Barzal.

Barzal was a healthy scratch for the next five games and then played once more before being sent back to the Seattle Thunderbirds of the Western Hockey League, who had drafted the Coquitlam, British

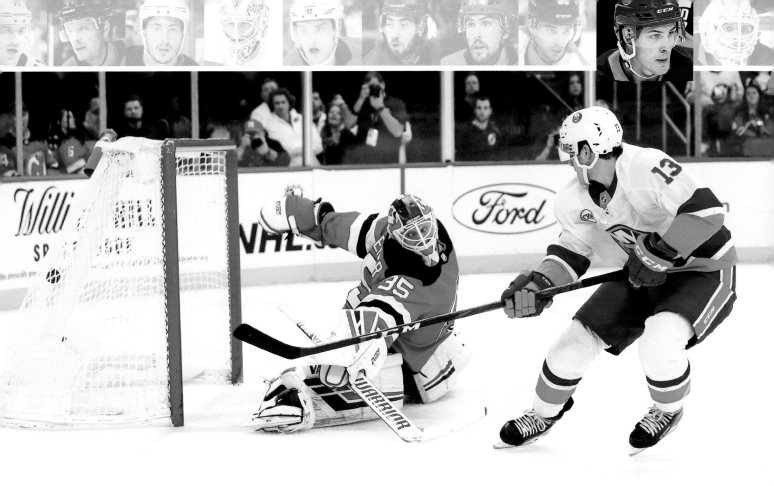

Winnipeg. "He sees the ice really well and he's skilled. He's got all the assets."

Barzal's numbers were down in 2018–19, to 18 goals and 62 points, but he was the driving force behind one of the more satisfying moments of a resurgent season for the Islanders under new coach Barry Trotz.

Facing their former captain John Tavares for the first time after he chose his hometown Toronto Maple Leafs in free agency, Barzal had a natural hat trick in less than eight minutes on the way to a 4–0 victory. He was the first Islander with a hat trick against Toronto since Mike Bossy in 1986.

Barzal, who took over Tavares' plum spot in the dressing room at the team's practice facility, harbors no ill will toward the departed superstar. "Seeing John the last two years helped me grow, just seeing how

he handles everything," he said. "He's such a pro. I learned a lot."

Islanders fans were a little less gracious about the loss and enjoyed a measure of revenge by finishing fourth in the conference, three points ahead of Toronto, and reaching the second round of the playoffs while the Maple Leafs were out in the first.

Barzal had seven points in eight postseason games, but his play was about more than numbers. He'd become more conscientious and "efficient," according to Trotz, which allowed Barzal to play more productive minutes.

"The one thing I like about Mathew — there's lots to like about Mathew, actually — is that he's a young player who plays fearless, probably just played on instinct and now he's starting to connect some dots on how important it is for responsibilities without the puck," said Trotz of the 22-year-old sophomore center.

Tavares played 82 NHL games the year he was drafted and it took Barzal two years to get there, but during their 20- and 21-year-old seasons Tavares just edged Barzal in points, 148 to 147. In major trophies, however, Barzal has the 1–0 shutout.

Won gold at the 2014 Hlinka Gretzky Cup

Named WHL playoff MVP in 2017

Won the Calder Trophy in 2018

Played in the 2019 NHL All-Star Game

93 ♠

MIKA ZIBANEJAD

METROPOLITAN DIVISION | Rangers | Center

Huddinge, just south of Stockholm.

The younger Zibanejad played for Djurgarden's under-18 and under-20 teams before making his debut in the Swedish Hockey League in 2010 at 17. The following season, at just 18 years and 172 days old, he played in his first NHL game, becoming the youngest Swede ever to play in an NHL game and the youngest player in Sens history.

After nine games the Senators sent Zibanejad back to Djurgarden, and at the 2012 World Junior Championship he scored the golden goal in overtime to give Sweden a 1–0 victory over Russia and the country's first World Junior title in 31 years.

NHL players were locked out to start the 2012–13 season, so Zibanejad started the year with the American Hockey League's Binghamton Senators. Called up when the season began, he scored his first NHL goal on January 30, 2013. He opened the following season in Binghamton again but was called up after scoring seven points in six games and stuck in the NHL for good.

In 2015–16 Zibanejad posted career highs in games played (81), goals (21), assists (30) and points (51). Then in the summer of 2016, just days after he'd moved into a new home, the Senators shocked Zibanejad by trading him to the New York Rangers for Derek Brassard.

Zibanejad embraced big city life and the relative anonymity that Manhattan affords a hockey player. The move was also popular with his friends back home, who were more familiar with the Original Six franchise that had Swedish legend Henrik Lundqvist minding the net.

Zibanejad had 15 points in his first 19 games with the Rangers before breaking his left fibula in November 2016, costing him 25 games. The following November he suffered a concussion that put him out of the lineup for nine games, so it was satisfying to play all 82 games in 2018–19.

The Ottawa Senators drafted Mika Zibanejad sixth overall in 2011, though that didn't impress his father much.

"Yesterday we enjoyed it, but that was yesterday and today we go back to business and take care of the plan for the future," said his dad, Mehrdad, an IT engineer with the Swedish government.

Mehrdad lived through the Iranian revolution in 1979 and was jailed for writing against it. He was then forced to fight in the Iran/Iraq war as part of his mandatory military service, so he has a more nuanced perspective than most hockey parents.

After Mehrdad had fulfilled his military obligation he immigrated to Sweden in 1983, where he met his Finnish-born wife, Ritva. Mika was born in 1993 in

The 6-foot-2, 213-pound Zibanejad reached the 30-goal plateau for the first time, becoming the first Rangers center to get there since Eric Lindros in 2001–02. He had 74 points, 23 more than his previous career best, and he also set career highs in assists, average ice time, shots on goal, faceoff wins and takeaways.

Zibanejad, who was named an alternate captain prior to the season, led the team in goals, assists, points, power-play goals, power-play assists, power-play points, shots on goal, takeaways and faceoff wins. He also had a hand in 10 consecutive goals scored by the Rangers, from January 19 to February 4, the first player in franchise history to do so.

The Rangers media voted Zibanejad team MVP, and he earned the Steven McDonald Extra Effort Award from fans, named after an NYPD officer who was paralyzed when he was shot on the job. McDonald presented the first award in 1988 until his death in 2017.

"It's a big honor, obviously," said Zibanejad, who joined Rangers luminaries Adam Graves, Mark Messier, Brian Leetch, Wayne Gretzky and Lundqvist as the only players to win both awards in the same season. "Not being here for that long, but very quickly I understood what it means, how much it means to the fans and the city and what the family name stands for. A huge honor and a lot of respect to them and a lot of respect to everyone here."

If there's one thing the award reminded Zibanejad, which his father has always known, it's that there's more to life than hockey.

Scored the overtime goal to win gold at the 2012 World Junior Championship

Won gold at the 2018 World Championship

Became the first Ranger with a point on 10 straight team goals (2018–19)

Voted Rangers MVP and the Steven McDonald Extra Effort Award winner in 2018–19

JUSTIN FAULK

METROPOLITAN DIVISION | Hurricanes | Defense

heart attack at only 37. It suddenly made the game of hockey seem a lot less serious.

"Disappointments to a normal kid weren't really a disappointment to him, because he had a true tragedy," said Gail. "It changes your level. When he was younger and a kid would be crying after they lost, he didn't understand that. It's just a game. Why are these little kids crying? Well, he was the same age as them, but he had been through something much worse in life."

After playing for South St. Paul High School Faulk spent two seasons with the U.S. National Team Development Program, where he set a single-season record for goals by a defenseman with 21. That convinced the Carolina Hurricanes to choose him 37th overall at the 2010 NHL Entry Draft.

As a University of Minnesota Duluth freshman the following season, Faulk led the team's defensemen with eight goals and 25 assists as the Bulldogs won their first NCAA Division I title.

It was Faulk's only season of collegiate hockey. He signed an entry-level contract with the Hurricanes in 2011 and had established himself as a regular by 2013–14. Since then he's become the team's best two-way defenseman and power-play quarterback, with a heavy shot from the point and Norris Trophy potential.

Faulk peaked with 34 assists and 49 points in 2014–15 and started the following year with 12 straight power-play goals by December, tying the franchise record for a season.

For three straight years, from 2015 to 2017, Faulk was Carolina's brightest light and All-Star Game representative. But after the Hurricanes shipped out their top goal-scorer in Jeff Skinner in 2018 it appeared Faulk might be part of the housecleaning.

Instead, with new owner Tom Dundon and coach Rod Brind'Amour in place, Faulk was made an alter-

Growing up in South St. Paul, Minnesota, Justin Faulk was a thoughtful, meticulous kid. As little more than an infant he would sit quietly to watch his older brother David's hockey games, not moving until the Zamboni had done its rounds. At home he'd follow alongside as his father, Dale, cut the grass until the job was done.

Another example of rapid maturation was his skating. As can be expected Faulk's first attempt, when he was 3 years old, was a failure. But when he tried again just a few months later he was suddenly a natural. His mother, Gail, attributed that to repeated viewings of *The Mighty Ducks*.

Already a serious child Faulk was forced to grow up even faster at the age of 7, when his father died of a

nate to captain Justin Williams to start the 2018–19 season. Having been named co-captain with Jordan Staal in 2017 by departed coach Bill Peters, it was a change in regime that changed everything in the room and took some weight off of Faulk.

It also brought the team's Storm Surge celebrations that propelled the Hurricanes into a wild-card berth. It was Faulk's first taste of the playoffs after eight seasons and 559 games in the NHL. "We had some gray, cloudy days," he said, not ironically.

The Canes upset the defending Stanley Cup champion Washington Capitals in the first round and in a second-round sweep of the New York Islanders Faulk scored his first postseason goal. It was a memorable one: he stepped out of the penalty box, caught a puck in the air over his shoulder, put it down while staying onside, and went backhand roof over Vezina Trophy finalist Robin Lehner.

It was "gross," according to teammate Warren Foegele, who flipped Faulk the puck. "An incredible goal."

Carolina's Cinderella run came to an end at the hands of the Boston Bruins in the Eastern Conference Final, but it didn't weigh as heavily on Faulk as on some of his teammates. He knows what real loss feels like.

"Not everything's perfect, not everything's the way you want it to be," said Faulk. "If things don't go well, there's another day to move on, get better. That's hockey, life, whatever. Learn from things, grow from things."

Won bronze at the 2011 World Junior Championship

Won the NCAA Division I championship in 2011

Named to the NHL All-Rookie Team in 2012

Won bronze at the 2013 and 2015 World Championship

Played in three NHL All-Star Games (2015, 2016, 2017)

SHAYNE GOSTISBEHERE

METROPOLITAN DIVISION | Flyers | Defense

Say what you will about commissioner Gary Bettman's Great Southern Experiment in terms of fan engagement and franchise solvency, but it is starting to produce high-end talent from some unlikely places.

Shayne Gostisbehere was born in Pembroke Pines, Florida, in 1993, the same year the Florida Panthers came into the NHL. His father, Regis, had moved there from France to play jai alai (a sport in which a ball is bounced off a walled court using a curved handheld device), and he met his French-Canadian bride-to-be, Christine, working at a jai alai court.

Shayne's sister took figure skating lessons at the Panthers' training facility, and he would tag along. He eventually stuck around the rink as a member of the Junior Panthers. His dad knew little about the game, so his grandfather, Denis, helped out. "I bought him a helmet, got him into a league and coached him for years before [former Panther] Ray Sheppard took over," said Denis. "He was always the smallest kid on the team, but I told him there are two things he has to remember: 'Let your stick and skates do the talking and no one will turn you down.'"

With his grandfather's wise words in mind, Gostisbehere left Florida to play hockey at South Kent School in Connecticut for his final two years of high school. He had 36 points in 24 games as a senior but went undrafted in 2011. Philadelphia took a flyer on Ghost in the 2012 draft, choosing him in the third round, 78th overall, after his first season at Union College in Schenectady, New York.

The Flyer scouts earned their pay. Gostisbehere won a gold medal with Team USA at the 2013 World Juniors, and in 2014 he was named Frozen Four MVP as Union won its first national championship. In the title game at Philadelphia's Wells Fargo Center he had a goal and two assists and was plus-7 in a 7–4 win over the University of Minnesota.

Flyers fans would have to wait for him to light up the rink again, however. After five games with the Lehigh Valley Phantoms of the American Hockey League, Gostisbehere tore his ACL and was lost for a year. He started the 2015–16 season with the Phantoms and finished it with the Flyers, coming second in Calder Trophy voting, ahead of Connor McDavid. "It definitely caught me by surprise," said Gostisbehere. "Nobody goes into their first few NHL games and expects to make such a splash."

Still undersized, Gostisbehere used his speed and creativity to score 17 goals and 46 points, 18 of which came during a 15-game point streak, the longest by

a rookie defenseman in NHL history and matching the longest by any defenseman since Chris Chelios in 1995. The last point of the streak was an overtime winner against the Toronto Maple Leafs, which made him the first rookie in history to score four overtime goals in a season.

Gostisbehere played in the 2016 NHL All-Star Game and was named to the All-Rookie Team. He was selected for the 23-and-under Team North America squad at the 2016 World Cup of Hockey, where he had four assists to tie for the team lead in points.

In his second season, however, Gostisbehere came back down to earth, a victim of the dreaded sophomore slump. The rookie phenom ended up watching games from the press box as a healthy scratch before picking up his play late in the season.

It's become the theme of Gostisbehere's career. After 65 points in 2017–18, which was fourth among all defensemen, just two points behind second and two ahead of Norris Trophy winner Victor Hedman, to go along with

elite possession metrics, he crashed back to earth with 37 points in 2018–19.

Gostisbehere's decline was especially precipitous on the power play, dropping from 33 points to 14. Being hampered by an early season knee injury wasn't an excuse, he insisted, but when confidence is lost, especially on defense, it's hard to regain. It didn't help that the Flyers were in turmoil; both general manager Ron Hextall and head coach Dave Hakstol were fired and the team failed to make the playoffs.

"I learned a lot about myself mentally, [but] it was a grind this season," said Gostisbehere. "I think finding that consistency, that sweet spot, it's going to be what I'm searching for this summer."

Won gold at the 2013 World Junior Championship

Won the NCAA championship and named Frozen Four MVP in 2014

Set the NHL record for longest point streak by a rookie defenseman (15 games)

Holds the NHL rookie record with four overtime goals in a season

Played in the 2016 NHL All-Star Game

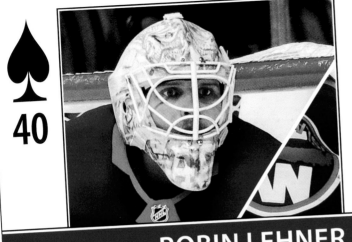

ROBIN LEHNER

METROPOLITAN DIVISION | Islanders | Goalie

SIGNED
Chicago Blackhawks
on July 1, 2019

he played for Sweden at the Under-18 World Championship before the Ottawa Senators chose him in the second round of the 2009 NHL draft.

Leaving Sweden, Lehner joined the Ontario Hockey League's Sault Ste. Marie Greyhounds in 2009–10 and played two games for the Senators' American Hockey League affiliate in Binghamton, winning both.

On January 13, 2011, Lehner made his NHL debut at 19 years and 173 days old, becoming the youngest goalie in franchise history. He spent most of that season in the AHL and led Binghamton to the Calder Cup with a 14-4 record, a 2.10 goals-against average and a .939 save percentage in the playoffs, capturing the Jack A. Butterfield Trophy as playoff MVP.

Lehner shuttled between Ottawa and Binghamton through the 2012–13 season and played 61 NHL games over the next two years. He missed the final 27 regular-season games of the 2014–15 season and the playoffs with a concussion before being traded to the Sabres.

W hile tending goal for the Buffalo Sabres on March 29, 2018, Robin Lehner thought he was having a heart attack. He was fatigued and short of breath and felt a crushing weight on his chest.

At the second intermission Lehner pulled himself from the game, but instead of going to the hospital he went home and did what he always did. He drank.

The native of Gothenburg, Sweden, had a tumultuous and troubled childhood, and didn't even try playing in net until he was 10. It came pretty easily to him though, and just five years later he was on Sweden's under-16 team and playing for his hometown Frolunda in the Swedish Hockey League's under-18 division.

Lehner backstopped Frolunda's under-20 team to a championship in 2008, and the following season

It was an equally rocky start in Buffalo. Lehner went down with a high ankle sprain in the season opener and missed 39 games in 2015–16. He set a career high with 59 games played in 2016–17 and had 129 starts and 42 wins over three seasons for the Sabres before his life changed with the panic attack that March night late in the 2017–18 season.

Knowing that if he didn't seek help he would die, either through abusing substances or by his own hand, Lehner left the team with the blessing of Sabres general manager Jason Botterill and the support of the NHL and NHLPA.

Lehner went to a treatment center in Arizona where he detoxed and was diagnosed with bipolar 1 with manic phases. He learned how growing up around addicts had shaped him, and he felt a kinship with

members of the military who were suffering from post-traumatic stress disorder.

After two months Lehner returned home to family, a stronger, healthier man, but one without a job.

Alongside his agent Lehner had some harrowing interviews with NHL general managers as he looked to find a place in an NHL crease. They didn't know his diagnosis so they questioned his character, unknowingly repeating back to him all the horrible things he'd felt about himself.

Lehner withstood that crucible and found his fresh start and a clean slate under the new regime on Long Island. President of hockey operations Lou Lamoriello and head coach Barry Trotz, two wise and savvy hockey men who have sipped from Lord Stanley's mug, gave him a one-year deal to prove himself. It worked out better than either party could have hoped.

Won the Calder Cup in 2011 and named AHL playoff MVP

Shared the William M. Jennings Trophy with Thomas Greiss in 2019

Voted a finalist for the Vezina Trophy in 2019

Awarded the Masterton Trophy in 2019

In 2018–19 Lehner was second in the NHL with a .930 save percentage, and his 2.13 goals-against average was third, one spot above goalie partner Thomas Greiss' 2.28. They shared the William M. Jennings Trophy after the Islanders allowed the fewest goals in the NHL, at 191, a year after allowing the most.

Lehner was one of three finalists for the Vezina Trophy, and he won the Masterton Trophy, given to the player who best exemplifies perseverance, sportsmanship and dedication to hockey. In his speech he said, "I'm not ashamed to say I'm mentally ill, but that doesn't mean I'm mentally weak."

The Islanders swept the Pittsburgh Penguins in the first round, but that wasn't Lehner's biggest win of the year. "Today, I am here a happy man, that is for the first time," he wrote in a personal essay in *The Athletic* prior to the season, "trying to live in the moment, day to day."

And he proved it, betting on himself and surprising many by signing a one-year contract with the Chicago Blackhawks. "I'm 27 turning 28," said Lehner, "and I truly in my soul know I am just scratching the surface."

CENTRAL DIVISION

FIRST TEAM

84	**PATRICK KANE**	Blackhawks	Right Wing
86	**NATHAN MacKINNON**	Avalanche	Center
88	**MARK SCHEIFELE**	Jets	Center
90	**ROMAN JOSI**	Predators	Defense
92	**JOHN KLINGBERG**	Stars	Defense
94	**PEKKA RINNE**	Predators	Goalie

SECOND TEAM

96	**TYLER SEGUIN**	Stars	Center
98	**JONATHAN TOEWS**	Blackhawks	Center
100	**BLAKE WHEELER**	Jets	Right Wing
102	**ALEX PIETRANGELO**	Blues	Defense
104	**P.K. SUBBAN**	Predators	Defense
106	**BEN BISHOP**	Stars	Goalie

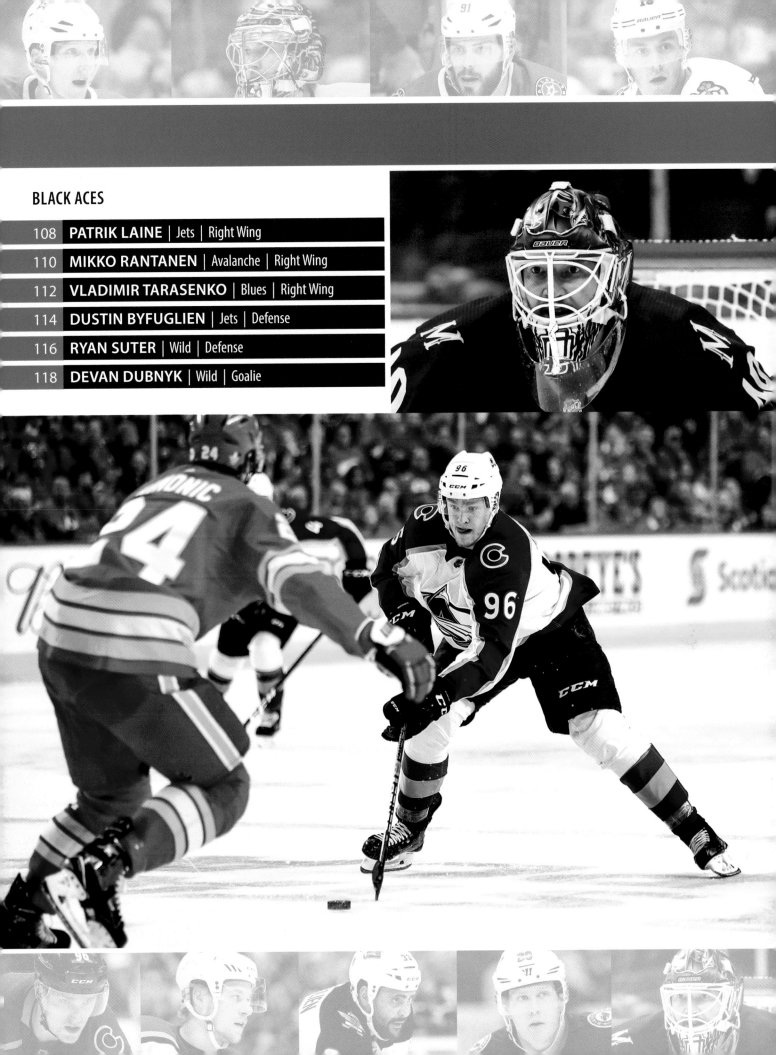

BLACK ACES

108	**PATRIK LAINE**	Jets	Right Wing
110	**MIKKO RANTANEN**	Avalanche	Right Wing
112	**VLADIMIR TARASENKO**	Blues	Right Wing
114	**DUSTIN BYFUGLIEN**	Jets	Defense
116	**RYAN SUTER**	Wild	Defense
118	**DEVAN DUBNYK**	Wild	Goalie

PATRICK KANE

Won the Calder Trophy in 2008

Played in eight NHL All-Star Games
(2009, 2011, 2012, 2015, 2016, 2017, 2018, 2019)

Won the Stanley Cup three times (2010, 2013, 2015)

Voted the Conn Smythe Trophy winner in 2013

Won the Hart Trophy, Art Ross Trophy and Ted Lindsay
Award in 2016

Patrick Kane is the product of working-class South Buffalo, where there's a "special culture," according to NHL icon Scotty Bowman, former coach and general manager of the Sabres. "If you're from South Buffalo — or you're accepted there — you're a different kind of guy."

Generously listed at 5-foot-10 and 177 pounds now, Kane was always the smallest and usually the best on his team. By the age of 11 he was putting up 230 points in a 60-game season. At 14 he had 160 points in 70 games for the Detroit HoneyBaked AAA team. Twice cut by the U.S. National Team Development Program because of his size, Kane broke a program record in his second season with 102 points in 58 games. In 2006–07, his lone season in the Ontario Hockey League, he had 62 goals and 145 points in 58 games for the London Knights. He was both the Canadian Hockey League's leading scorer and Rookie of the Year.

After being drafted first overall by the Chicago Blackhawks in 2007, Kane stepped right into the NHL and had 21 goals and 72 points to win the Calder Trophy. It was the Blackhawks' first winning season in six years and the start of a resurgence that culminated in three Stanley Cups.

In 2010 Kane had 10 goals and 28 points in 22 playoff games, the last of which in Game 6 against the Philadelphia Flyers made him the youngest player to score the Stanley Cup–winning goal in overtime.

Kane's nine goals and 19 points in the 2013 play-offs earned him the Conn Smythe Trophy as the Blackhawks brought another championship back to Chicago, and in 2015 he came back from a broken collarbone to score 23 points in 23 playoff games to win his third Stanley Cup.

But troubled times were ahead. In August 2015 Kane was accused of sexual assault at his lake house outside of Buffalo. While the district attorney declined to press charges it wasn't forgotten in opposing rinks, especially in his hometown.

Kane had already pleaded guilty to noncriminal

disorderly conduct as a result of assaulting a cab driver in 2009, and the people of Buffalo had run out of patience with their wayward child and weren't afraid to voice it when the Blackhawks came to town.

Either Kane is adept at compartmentalizing or the anger directed at him was motivation in 2015–16. He had a 26-game point streak and in his lone game in Buffalo he tied the score with 35.9 seconds left and then beat the Sabres with a shootout goal.

After leading the NHL that season with 106 points (46 goals, 60 assists), 17 more than second-place Jamie Benn, Kane became the first American-born player to win the Art Ross and Hart trophies. He completed the hat trick with the Ted Lindsay Award.

These are a few of the reasons why in 2017 Kane was named one of the NHL's 100 Greatest Players ever, one of only six active players to make the list, and he continues to pad his résumé.

After leading the 2018 World Championship in scoring with 20 points in 10 games and being named MVP, Kane had 44 goals and career highs in assists (66) and points (110) in 2018–19. He was third in NHL scoring and a finalist for the Ted Lindsay Award.

His skill is undeniable, but one of the reasons Kane has and will continue to put up these numbers is another Gretzky-esque quality — elusiveness. Already slender and shifty like the Great One, he had prepared for the season by focusing on flexibility and mobility instead of strength. Down 12 pounds he'd made it even harder for opponents to zero in on him and his point total went up by 34. He also averaged a career high 22:29 of ice time.

"He's one of those guys who shows up early, stays late, does everything he's supposed to do, always," said trainer Ian Mack. "He can tell you what he's eating next Wednesday at 10:30 a.m. He knows how many hours he's going to sleep."

Credit Kane for maturity and choosing the gym instead of the bars of Buffalo; early in his career he didn't even know where he was going to sleep.

NATHAN MacKINNON

The town of Cole Harbour, Nova Scotia, has about 25,000 residents and probably the highest quotient of hockey talent per capita on the planet. Not only did the town produce Sidney Crosby, one of the best players to ever grace NHL ice, but it also gave the world Nathan MacKinnon.

MacKinnon put skates on at just 2 years old. His father, Graham, a former goalie, set up the garage as a "shooting gallery," according to his mom, Kathy.

"He wouldn't put the pads on — his knees are too bad for that," said Nathan, recalling his games with his dad. "But he'd get in there and use his feet to stop my shots when I was little. But then I learned how to lift it and he couldn't play net anymore."

As he did with his father's aged goaltending skills,

MacKinnon quickly outgrew the local hockey scene. Still just 14, he left Cole Harbour to attend Shattuck-St. Mary's in Minnesota, the same school that Crosby played for.

After two years at boarding school MacKinnon came home to play for the Quebec Major Junior Hockey League's Halifax Mooseheads, about 10 miles west of Cole Harbour. "We had it in our heads that when he went to Shattuck, he probably wouldn't ever be home again," said Kathy. "I had convinced myself then that I had to get used to it. But when it came to be that he'd be playing in Halifax, that was a real treat."

MacKinnon led the Mooseheads to their first Memorial Cup in 2013, scoring seven goals and six assists in four games to take home the Stafford Smythe Memorial Trophy as tournament MVP.

Another Cole Harbour quality is the ability to rise to the occasion. Against the Portland Winterhawks and Seth Jones, the top-ranked skater in the upcoming entry draft, MacKinnon had a hat trick in a win in the preliminary round. Facing them again in the final, he had another hat trick, including an empty-netter to clinch the title.

Jones ended up going fourth to the Nashville Predators in the 2013 NHL Entry Draft. The Colorado Avalanche picked MacKinnon first overall.

MacKinnon made his Avalanche debut at 18 years and 31 days old, making him the youngest player in franchise history. He finished the 2013–14 season leading all rookies in assists (39) and points (63) and tied for most goals (24). He also had three assists in Game 1 of the first playoff round against the Minnesota Wild to become the first rookie in history to accomplish that feat in his playoff debut. He capped the season off by becoming the youngest player (at 18 years and 224 days old) to win the Calder Trophy.

The next few seasons were a little bleak, despite MacKinnon's best efforts. He led the last place Avalanche in scoring in 2016–17 and was their only representative at the 2017 NHL All-Star Game, but Colorado missed the playoffs for the third straight year.

In 2017–18 MacKinnon jumped all the way to fifth in the NHL in scoring with 97 points, and the Avalanche made the playoffs for the first time since 2014. A year later he was tied for sixth in goals (41) and seventh in points (99), one point behind Crosby, and he took it to another level in the 2019 postseason.

"MacKinnon is a guy that for me is probably the most fun to watch right now," said Connor McDavid during the playoffs. "He is so dynamic, so fast, I mean his hands are so fast, too. Just the way he plays the game, the only word that comes to mind is dynamic when he plays. It's been pretty cool to see."

And Crosby added, "He's definitely doing it all out there and has the puck all the time. He's dominating."

MacKinnon had 13 points in 12 playoff games, and several of his six goals were of the did-you-just-see-that variety. His speed tore the top-seeded Calgary Flames apart in the first round before the Avalanche fell to the San Jose Sharks in the second.

MacKinnon has called on his Cole Harbour elder and partner in Canadian coffee shop commercials to get advice on playoff hockey, and the two still skate together in the off-season. The mentorship is one of the reasons the 24-year-old has reached the NHL's upper echelon, but until he gets his hands on the Stanley Cup he'll remain in Crosby's shadow.

As MacKinnon himself says, "Players aren't remembered for what they do in the regular season."

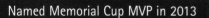

Named Memorial Cup MVP in 2013

Selected first overall in the 2013 NHL Entry Draft

Won the 2014 Calder Trophy, the youngest player ever to win it

Won gold at the 2015 World Championship

Played in three NHL All-Star Games (2017, 2018, 2019)

MARK SCHEIFELE

Mark Scheifele is a hockey nerd. Although he's tired of the label, it fits, and it's the reason he's climbed the NHL ladder.

Growing up in Kitchener, Ontario, Scheifele was sports obsessed. "He would sit in this big white chair in the living room, eating his cereal as he was watching *SportsCentre*," said his father, Brad.

All three Scheifele kids played sports, but Mark was the most serious and the most competitive. "I was always the worst loser," he recalled. "Anytime I lost it was a big ordeal . . . I just couldn't stand for losing."

The drive was inborn, not taught. The Scheifele parents insisted their children play multiple sports and have fun in each of them. Mark played hockey, soccer, lacrosse, volleyball and track and field, and

he left a trail of broken equipment when things didn't go his way. Never his precious hockey sticks, though.

Scheifele didn't focus on hockey until he was 16. He was chosen in the seventh round of the Ontario Hockey League draft by the Saginaw Spirit in 2009 but was sent home after training camp.

Back in Kitchener with the Junior B Dutchmen, Scheifele had 55 points in 51 games and was the league's rookie of the year. His OHL rights were then acquired by the Barrie Colts, where coach Dale Hawerchuk — Winnipeg's first overall draft pick in 1981, a former Jets captain and a Hall of Fame inductee — convinced him to learn and grow under his tutelage.

The Colts finished last in the OHL in 2010–11, but Scheifele had 75 points in 66 games and climbed into the low first round in NHL draft rankings. A few eyebrows were raised when the Jets picked him seventh overall in 2011, their first selection after the franchise had relocated from Atlanta. Winnipeg scouts Marcel Comeau and Mark Hillier went out on a limb for Scheifele. Management knew he wasn't going to stroll right into the NHL as an 18-year-old, but they believed he had the work ethic to get there and the humility to realize he'd need it.

Scheifele's first NHL game was also the reborn Jets' first since returning to Manitoba, and his first goal came four games later, in front of family in Toronto, against the Maple Leafs on October 19, 2011. It was his only point in 11 regular-season games with the Jets over his first two seasons; the rest were back in Barrie, where he had 142 points in 92 combined games.

In 2013–14 Scheifele stuck with the Jets permanently and slowly moved up the depth chart at center over the next two seasons. Then in early 2016, after inheriting the first-line role, Scheifele showed what he was truly capable of. In 82 games between January 2016 and January 2017, his 85 points trailed only Sidney Crosby and Connor McDavid.

Scheifele played on Team North America's top line at the 2016 World Cup of Hockey with McDavid and Auston Matthews, the first overall draft picks in 2015 and 2016, respectively. The immediate success of these two teenagers was a contrast to 23-year-old Scheifele's comparatively long road to stardom.

After Scheifele finished 2016–17 with 32 goals and 82 points, good for seventh in the league, he was limited to 60 games in 2017–18. He still managed to get 60 points, and he picked that pace up in the postseason, with 14 goals and 20 points in 17 playoff games as the Jets made it to the Western Conference Final. Along the way Scheifele set records for most away goals in a single series, with seven against the Nashville Predators, and most away goals in one post-season, with 11.

Back to full health and schedule in 2018–19, Scheifele had 38 goals and 84 points and played in his first All-Star Game. After five points in six games during Winnipeg's early postseason exit, Kitchener Clutch now has 36 goals and 80 points in 70 career playoff games in the OHL, AHL and NHL.

Not many saw him becoming the center on the Jets' top line and first power-play unit, with three consecutive point-per-game seasons and counting, but not all NHL stars are born. Some are created with time and utter devotion to the game.

"I don't think there could ever be a day in my life where hockey's not a part of it," said Scheifele. "I literally live and breathe hockey and it's the love of my life."

Spoken like a true nerd.

Won bronze at the 2012 World Junior Championship

Finished seventh in NHL scoring with 82 points in 2016–17

Won gold at the 2016 World Championship

Won silver at the 2017 World Championship

Played in the 2019 NHL All-Star Game

ROMAN JOSI

Won silver at the 2013 and 2018 World Championship

Named best defender and MVP of the 2013 World Championship

Played in two NHL All-Star Games (2016, 2019)

Named eighth captain in franchise history in 2017

Nashville Predators defenseman Roman Josi played forward until he was 14, and only two years after moving back to the blue line the native of Bern, Switzerland, joined SC Bern in the country's top division. It takes elite talent to ascend that quickly, which he had in his DNA.

"My mother was a swimmer on the national team, and my father was a top-level footballer," explained Josi. "When I first started, I didn't really mind how I played. It wasn't that important. But when the first agents started to show up, I was 15, and I realized that hockey was big business."

The Predators drafted Josi in the second round, 38th overall, in 2008. He spent two more years in Switzerland before coming to North America and playing for the Milwaukee Admirals, Nashville's American Hockey League affiliate, when he was 20.

Josi made his NHL debut in the 2011–12 season, and by his second year he was already on the team's top pairing. He followed that season up by leading the underdog Swiss to the 2013 World Championship final against host Sweden.

Josi had Switzerland's only goal in the final, one of his four goals and nine points in the tournament. He took home the top defenseman and MVP awards to go with his silver medal.

In 2013–14 Josi became a serious offensive threat in the NHL with 13 goals and 40 points, and the following season he was up to 55 points.

When captain and franchise icon Shea Weber was traded in 2016 Josi took on the roles of shutdown defender and defensive anchor that his former partner had held. He emerged from Weber's shadow and started getting the recognition he deserved, but the flashy P.K. Subban was added in the trade.

Josi is also so positionally and fundamentally sound that he doesn't stand out. He's efficient, effective and complete, with metronomic steadiness.

Averaging more ice time than anyone on the team in 2016–17, Josi helped the Predators squeak into the playoffs as the eighth seed and then sweep the

top-seeded Chicago Blackhawks on the way to the franchise's first Western Conference championship and trip to the Stanley Cup Final. He had six goals and 14 points in 22 playoff games, which was second on the team and among NHL defensemen in scoring. His consistency also gave partner Ryan Ellis the confidence to take chances and become a postseason star.

When Mike Fisher retired after the season it was an easy decision for coaches and management to stitch the C on Josi's jersey.

From 2014–15 to 2018–19 Josi's 274 points tied for third among NHL defensemen with Victor Hedman. He tied for fifth in goals (70) and power-play goals (25), and was sixth in average ice time (25:21) and seventh in points per game (0.7).

With one year left on his team-friendly contract, the 29-year-old is a star in his prime and due for a raise. For Predators goalie Pekka Rinne, who has benefitted from the acumen of the 6-foot-1, 201-pound defender

in front of him, re-signing him at any cost is a no-brainer, for the present and future of the franchise.

"For a younger guy, if you follow him, you're on a pretty good track," said Rinne. "Pay attention to what he does on and off the ice. Not only that, to me he's our best player."

But it's not just in the Predators' dressing room that he garners respect. Writing in *The Players' Tribune* the San Jose Sharks' Logan Couture named Josi one of the five toughest defensemen he's ever played against, and the Winnipeg Jets' Mark Scheifele singled him out in "The 5 Toughest Players I've Ever Faced."

"He'll beat you senseless for the 30 seconds you're in their zone — and then when Nashville gains possession, he'll jump up as the fourth man in the rush," wrote Scheifele. "That's rare: Usually guys who play with that kind of an edge in the d-zone don't have the energy to jump up into the rush. I don't know how he does it."

JOHN KLINGBERG

Won gold at the 2012 World Junior Championship

Named to the NHL All-Rookie Team in 2014–15

Led all NHL defensemen in assists and was second in points in 2017–18

Won gold at the 2017 and 2018 World Championship

Played in the 2018 NHL All-Star Game

It took guts for John Klingberg, as a fifth-round draft pick, to say no to Dallas Stars general manager Jim Nill.

After being selected 131st overall in 2010, Nill wanted Klingberg to come play in the American Hockey League in 2013–14, but the straightforward Swede told his boss he thought he'd be better served in the Swedish Hockey League. And so it was.

Klingberg had his reasons; he'd joined Jokerit in Finland's top league, the Liiga, in 2011–12 and hated it. "I was too young to move away," he said.

The homesickness didn't last long, as Klingberg was back in Sweden by season's end, on loan to Skelleftea. Then in 2012–13, he suffered knee and hip injuries, so he honestly felt he could better refine his game and build his confidence with another year at home in Gothenburg, and he was right.

As a 21-year-old Klingberg played heavy minutes in all situations and had 28 points in 50 games for his hometown Frolunda in the SHL.

Klingberg came to North America to stay in 2014–15, and after 12 points in the first 10 games of the season with the AHL's Texas Stars, the NHL's Stars were convinced and called him up. He never played in the minors again.

In 65 games with Dallas in 2014–15 Klingberg set a team record for most goals (11), assists (29) and points (40) by a rookie defenseman. He was fifth in Calder Trophy voting after leading all rookie defensemen in assists and points and finishing fourth in assists and seventh in points among all first-year players.

Klingberg followed that up with seasons of 58 and 49 points and established himself as one of the league's top offensive defensemen. In 2017–18 Dallas brought back Ken Hitchcock behind the bench, and the notoriously defensive-minded coach worked with Klingberg on rounding out his game. Klingberg still had 59 assists to lead all NHL blue-liners and 67 points to tie for second in scoring among defensemen, but the added defensive dimension didn't go unnoticed and he finished sixth in Norris Trophy voting.

"He plays both ends of the ice, which most people probably don't see because he has such good numbers offensively," said St. Louis Blues defenseman Alex Pietrangelo, one of the players Klingberg looks up to and emulates. "Playing against him, he's a guy you circle. He's a guy who, once he touches the puck, something's going to happen every time."

Jim Montgomery was hired as the new Stars coach before the 2018–19 season and brought in a more free-flowing system that the slick Swede is quite happy to play in. Klingberg missed 18 games after having surgery to insert eight screws and two plates in his left hand but still had 10 goals and 45 points and set a career high with 24:32 of average ice time, good for 11th in the NHL.

In the regular season Klingberg was tied for second among NHL defensemen with five game-winning goals, and in his second trip to the postseason he scored the overtime goal in Game 6 of the opening round that eliminated the Nashville Predators.

Klingberg is the first defenseman in franchise history with at least 30 points in each of his first five seasons, and with 259 points in 367 games he's seventh in scoring among defensemen since entering the league.

Tall and lean at 6-foot-2 and 180 pounds, Klingberg is in the meaty part of his prime at the age of 27, and he's the ideal role model for 20-year-old Miro Heiskanen, the third overall draft pick in 2017 who made the All-Star Game in his rookie season.

One of the most important lessons Klingberg will impart is to keep growing and learning. He knows how competitive the NHL is and how hard it is to become established and move with the ever-evolving game.

"I have not stopped," said Klingberg. "I know what I can do. I know what I can be. Can I be that true number one defenseman?

"Can I do it year after year? I don't want to stop."

PEKKA RINNE

Led the NHL in wins (43), saves (1,987), games (73) and points (five) in 2011–12

Won silver at the 2014 World Championship and named tournament MVP

Named to four NHL All-Star Games (2015, 2016, 2018, 2019)

Won the Vezina Trophy in 2018

Wayne Gretzky once said there are three seasons: the regular season, the playoffs and the Stanley Cup Final. Pekka Rinne mastered the first two, but the third had a steeper learning curve. That he was even there, though, is remarkable.

There was no NHL coverage when Rinne was growing up in Kempele, Finland, but he spent Saturday mornings watching a highlight show and modeling his game on fellow Finn Miikka Kiprusoff and Hall of Famer Dominik Hasek in the winter, while sharpening his hand-eye coordination and reaction time playing pesapallo, a Finnish version of baseball in the summer.

Rinne was a little-known commodity when he was first eligible for the NHL Entry Draft in 2001. He was the backup goalie on the Liiga's Karpat Oulu and was passed over for three years.

In his fourth year of eligibility in 2004, the Nashville Predators drafted Rinne in the eighth round, 258th overall. The Predators only chose him because they were running out of players on their draft board and Helsinki-based scout Janne Kekalainen advocated for him. "You could easily tell he was mobile, but the most impressive thing was the energy, drive, sportsmanship oozing out of him," said Kekalainen.

Rinne joined the American Hockey League's Milwaukee Admirals for the 2005–06 season and spent three years there before cracking the Predators' lineup full-time.

In 2008–09 the 6-foot-5, 217-pound contortionist had 29 wins, a 2.38 goals-against average and a .917 save percentage to finish fourth in Calder Trophy voting. As a testament to his consistency, after 11 seasons Rinne's career goals-against average is the exact same as his rookie year's and his save percentage is .001 higher.

The 2010–11 season was Rinne's highest above this mean, with career bests in goals-against average (2.12) and save percentage (.930) to finish second in Vezina Trophy voting and fourth for the Hart Trophy.

But it was the 2017 postseason that was his finest hour. Facing the top-seeded Blackhawks in the opening round, Rinne stopped 59 shots over the first two games for back-to-back shutouts. He completed the sweep with an incredible .976 save percentage, including .991 in 5-on-5 play, and a 0.70 goals-against average.

Rinne also stole series-clinching Game 6 of the Western Conference Final despite the Predators being outshot 41-18 by the Anaheim Ducks. Nashville had reached the franchise's first Stanley Cup Final.

Game 1 showed that the final is a different beast, though. Entering with a .941 playoff save percentage, Rinne faced only 11 shots in a 5–3 loss to the Penguins for a .636 save percentage — the worst in recorded playoff history. He then allowed four goals in Game 2 and was pulled in a 4–1 defeat.

Rinne righted the ship from there and Conn Smythe Trophy talk was revived, but the Penguins won the series in six games.

There was no letdown the following season; Rinne posted a sparkling 42-13-4 record, with a 2.31 goals-against average, .927 save percentage and eight shutouts. The old playoff bugaboo returned though, as Rinne's struggles prompted backup and fellow Finn Juuse Saros into the net in the decisive Game 7 loss in the second round to the Winnipeg Jets.

"Listen to me, anyone who wants to criticize, critics who want to criticize him, [they] don't know what they're talking about," said former teammate P.K. Subban in 2018. "[Rinne] is the backbone of our hockey club and he's one of the main reasons we're here."

And in the fourth season — awards season — in his fourth time as a finalist, voters agreed, as Rinne won the 2018 Vezina Trophy.

After another consistent season in 2018–19 and a first-round loss to the Dallas Stars, the 36-year-old Rinne said he probably has two more seasons in him, when his current contract expires. All of them have been in Nashville and he's promised the city one thing.

"Eventually, I guarantee it — Nashville will win a Cup," he wrote after coming so close in 2017.

"All the great hockey towns do."

TYLER SEGUIN

Named the OHL's Most Outstanding Player in 2010

Won the Stanley Cup in 2011

Won the Spengler Cup in 2012

Played in five NHL All-Star Games (2012, 2015, 2016, 2017, 2018)

Won gold at the 2015 World Championship

"Thank you, Kessel" used to be a popular refrain from fans at Boston's TD Garden whenever the Toronto Maple Leafs visited the hometown Bruins.

The genesis of the taunt was the Leafs having traded two first-round draft picks to the Bruins as part of a package for Phil Kessel, the first of which became second overall pick Tyler Seguin in 2010.

Born in 1992 in Brampton, Ontario, Seguin attended the elite private school St. Michael's College in Toronto, which has produced scores of NHL players. Starting at the age of 13, he woke up at 5:30 each morning so he could catch a series of buses to get to school on time.

His father, Paul, who played hockey at the University of Vermont, didn't think an easy path and continued dominance over his local peers would serve his son well down the road. "I think a lot of what was done made Tyler stronger," said Paul. "We knew there were going to be challenges in his life and in hockey.

"I think every kid needs that. But he has this amazing ability to overcome challenges, whatever they are."

At 16, Tyler traveled even farther from home, playing in Michigan for the Plymouth Whalers of the Ontario Hockey League. He scored 69 goals and 173 points in 124 games over two seasons, igniting the great Taylor/Tyler debate for the 2010 NHL Entry Draft. The two tied for most points in the OHL in 2009–10, with Seguin winning the Red Tilson Trophy as the OHL's Most Outstanding Player. But it was Taylor Hall who was taken first overall by the Edmonton Oilers.

Constantly being compared to Hall and Kessel and playing under coach Claude Julien, who doesn't always trust young players, Seguin endured a difficult rookie season. He averaged only eight minutes a game, and the first time he dressed in the 2011 playoffs was for Game 1 of the Eastern Conference Final.

Seguin scored a nifty goal in his playoff debut and, finally unleashed, followed it the next game with another beauty, part of a four-point period. He had

three goals and seven points in 13 postseason games, as the Bruins went on to win the Stanley Cup.

Accused of immaturity, excessive partying and not fitting into Julien's defensive system, however, Seguin was only 21 when the Bruins sent him to the Dallas Stars, 10 days after they lost to the Chicago Blackhawks in the 2013 Cup final.

In his first year in Big D, Seguin was moved to center and given more offensive freedom. He formed one of the NHL's most productive partnerships alongside Jamie Benn with 84 points in 80 games.

"He was like any other 21-year-old," explained Stars general manager Jim Nill of Seguin's reputation when he made the trade. "He did some things he probably would like to take back, if you could, but you learn from it."

It's fair to say the Stars would make the trade again. Over his first six years in Dallas, from 2013–14 to 2018–19, Seguin had 206 goals and 464 points, tied for fifth in the NHL in both categories over that span,

and he's one of just three NHL players to have 70-plus points in each of those seasons. And while Seguin piles up the numbers he's also added a defensive dimension to his game, including killing penalties. It was more than enough to convince Dallas to sign him to an eight-year, $78.8 million contract in 2018.

After missing all but one game in the 2016 playoffs with a sliced Achilles, the last time Dallas qualified, Seguin played all 82 games in each of the next three seasons. His 33 goals and 80 points in 2018–19 led the Stars and helped them back to the postseason.

Seguin had 11 points in 13 playoff games but the St. Louis Blues beat the Stars in double overtime in Game 7 in the second round. It was a bitter defeat for a player who reached the summit early.

"The taste of it sticks with me, winning the Cup," said Seguin. "You'll never lose that taste.

"It's taken time to understand that. It's taken a lot of losing and not being in the playoffs to fully understand that. I have a much bigger appreciation for it."

JONATHAN TOEWS

Even his parents knew early on. "If I had not seen him being born, I would swear he's older," said his mother, Andrée Gilbert. And according to his father, Bryan, "He had been skating by the time he was three-and-a-half and had a stride at four. That blew my mind."

Jonathan Toews continued to mature quickly, with an adult's intensity long before puberty. Growing up in the St. Vital neighborhood in south Winnipeg, his team of 7-year-olds lost a tournament game to a team a year older. "He was so upset," said Bryan. "I tried to explain that the other team was all older boys, but he didn't accept that. He wanted to beat them."

Toews had the talent to match. He was chosen first overall in the 2003 Western Hockey League draft by the Tri-City Americans but decided to attend Shattuck-St. Mary's, the Minnesota prep school that produced Sidney Crosby, because it was closer to home and he'd remain eligible to play in the NCAA.

Serious about school, too, Toews completed three years of high school in two and enrolled at the University of North Dakota in 2005 at 17. He had 85 points in 76 games over two seasons with the Fighting Sioux and won gold at the World Junior Championship with Canada both years.

The second, in 2007, will be remembered for the win over Team USA in the semis, when Toews had three goals in three attempts in a seven-round shootout.

"He was so cool," said coach Craig Hartsburg. "Maybe on the inside, something else was going on, but not on the outside."

Toews was drafted third overall by the Chicago Blackhawks in 2006 and made his NHL debut in 2007 with that year's first overall pick, Patrick Kane. One prescient scout predicted Kane would one day lead the NHL in scoring, which he did, while Toews would lead the Blackhawks to the Stanley Cup, which he's done three times.

After being dubbed Mr. Serious by his Chicago teammates, Toews was upgraded to Captain Serious in 2008. He'd played only 64 NHL games and was then the third-youngest captain in league history.

Invited to Canada's Olympic orientation camp in 2009, Toews still wasn't sure he belonged: "I'm watching Sidney Crosby, a young captain like myself, and it's pretty incredible to see a guy who's about my age doing the things he's doing. I get praise for things that are modest compared to what he's done."

When the 2010 Olympics rolled around, Crosby got most of the headlines and the Golden Goal, but Toews led Canada in scoring and was named the tournament's best forward. A few months later he

had 29 points in 22 playoff games to win the Stanley Cup, the Blackhawks' first in 49 years. He became the second-youngest captain to lift the Cup, after Crosby, and the second-youngest player to be named playoff MVP, after Patrick Roy, when he was voted the Conn Smythe Trophy winner. He also became the youngest player in history to join the Triple Gold Club, with his Stanley Cup, Olympic gold and World Championship gold, which he'd won in 2007.

The general manager of the Olympic team was Steve Yzerman, the first-ballot Hall of Famer, whom Toews is most frequently compared to. Over 22 seasons Yzerman won three Stanley Cups, one Conn Smythe and one Selke Trophy. After winning two more Cups in 2013 and 2015 and the Selke in 2013, Toews had done all of that by the end of his eighth season. He then added the Mark Messier Leadership Award in 2015, another Olympic gold in 2014 and the World Cup of Hockey in 2016.

Always wise beyond his years Toews is now in his 30s and entering the back nine of his career. Even his most ardent fans would admit his play had declined

after so many miles put on with long playoff runs and international hockey, as well as nagging back problems. But after a career-low 52 points in 2017–18 he had a renaissance in 2018–19 with new highs in goals (35), assists (46) and points (81).

Running mate Kane also had a career year, making the Blackhawks' second straight season outside the playoff picture all the more frustrating. For a winner like Toews, that burns, but the fire is fuel for a return to Cup contention.

"That pain and that fear, that missing out, is a good thing," said Toews. "It just makes you hungrier."

Won gold at the 2006 and 2007 World Junior Championship, 2007 World Championship and 2010 and 2014 Olympics
Won the Stanley Cup three times (2010, 2013, 2015)
Won the Conn Smythe Trophy in 2010
Awarded the Frank J. Selke Trophy in 2013
Won the 2016 World Cup of Hockey

BLAKE WHEELER

CENTRAL DIVISION

Jets | Right Wing | 26

"Blake Wheeler is a leader in all phases of his life," according to Don Lucia, and he would know. Wheeler won a Minnesota state championship with his son in bantam and Lucia coached him in college.

"Blake was an extremely hard-working player on and off the ice," added Lucia. "He was humble and was a great teammate. He was a coach's dream, did everything I asked on the ice, in the weight room, in the classroom."

Wheeler grew up in the Minneapolis suburb Robbinsdale, where he led Breck School to a Class A state championship as a junior, scoring 45 regular-season goals and a hat trick in the final.

Drafted fifth overall by the Phoenix Coyotes in 2004, Wheeler played one season with the Green Bay Gamblers of the United States Hockey League before joining the University of Minnesota in 2005, where he scored one of the most memorable goals in NCAA history.

In overtime of the 2007 Western Collegiate Hockey Association championship game against North Dakota, Wheeler dove to prevent an icing call and while sliding on his stomach simultaneously roofed the puck with one hand to end the game. He was named tournament MVP.

Wheeler never signed with the Coyotes, so the Boston Bruins picked him up as a free agent in 2008.

Wheeler made a good first impression in Boston with 45 points in 2008–09, and his plus-36 was second in the NHL, but he wasn't given a consistent role or ice time and was dealt to the Atlanta Thrashers in 2011 at the trade deadline. The Bruins won the Stanley Cup that year, and the Thrashers moved to Winnipeg to become the second coming of the Jets.

"It helped me, gave me a kick in the rear a little bit," reflected Wheeler. "You know, you get traded from a team that wins the Stanley Cup, it's kind of a slap in the face."

Wheeler also believes working in the Winnipeg community and becoming a father helped him grow up and take his job more seriously.

"You start having to take care of the livelihood of your kids and it kind of kicks you in the butt a little bit," said Wheeler. "It sharpens your focus."

Described as a gangly teenager, Wheeler also took some time to grow into his body. Now 6-foot-5 and 225 pounds, he can and does play hard, but there's silk in his skating and softness in his hands.

Wheeler tied Claude Giroux for the league lead in assists in 2017–18 with 68 and led with 48 primary assists. He set a franchise record with assists in nine straight games along the way and joined Wayne Gretzky as the only player in history to record an assist on nine consecutive team goals. His 91 points were ninth in the NHL, and in the playoffs he led the Jets with 21 points in 17 games, including 18 assists. In a second-round victory over the Nashville Predators he had nine assists and 11 points in seven games.

Wheeler upped his assist total to 71 in 2018–19, good for third in the NHL, and since 2015–16 only Hart Trophy winner Connor McDavid has had more assists. Wheeler also had 20 goals, including four in a game against the Columbus Blue Jackets, his sixth straight season of at least 20.

Now 33 Wheeler is coming off the most productive years of his career with two straight seasons of 91 points, which put him 10th in the NHL over that span. Since the Jets came back to town in 2011 he leads the franchise with 569 points, almost 200 more than runner-up Mark Scheifele.

In that time Wheeler is also first in the NHL in assists (384) and third in points among right wingers, behind Patrick Kane and Phil Kessel.

Named Jets captain in 2016 Wheeler is an intense character who commands respect and affection from veterans and young stars alike.

"He is one of the finest captains that I've ever had," said coach Paul Maurice. "His consistency on a daily basis, his ability to drive, the impact he's had on our young players — our whole team — is invaluable for their development for the next 15 years."

Stated more simply by Matt Hendricks, a veteran leader in his own right who played for the Jets in 2017–18 and was brought back at the trade deadline in 2019: "I love Blake Wheeler."

Won the 2007 WCHA championship and was named tournament MVP

Scored four goals and named MVP of 2009 NHL YoungStars game

Tied for the NHL lead in assists (68) in 2017–18 and was first in primary assists (48)

Played in two NHL All-Star Games (2018, 2019)

ALEX PIETRANGELO

Alex Pietrangelo wears four rubber bands around his wrist when he plays, the colored kind that show support for a cause. There's a light-blue one for his niece Ellie, who beat kidney cancer; a dark-blue one for Liam, a 2-year-old heart transplant recipient he met in 2016; and then an orange one for Mandi Schwartz, sister of teammate Jaden Schwartz, and a blue and yellow one for Seth Lange, a St. Louis teenager, both of whom died of leukemia.

The last two bands on his wrist don't represent all the people he's lost. In 2001, on Pietrangelo's 11th birthday, his friend Cosmo Oppedisano succumbed to cancer. It was an early lesson of life's cruelty, in an otherwise idyllic childhood.

Pietrangelo spent his early days on a backyard rink in King City, 45 minutes north of Toronto, complete with outdoor lights, bonfires and best friends. But his talent soon outgrew his town and he joined the Toronto Junior Canadiens.

Facing the Markham Waxers at the 2005 all-Ontario bantam championship, Pietrangelo told nervous coach Tyler Cragg not to worry, just before the defenseman jumped over the boards and scored the game-winning goal. The two became friends, and Cragg continued to train Pietrangelo well into his NHL days, until he died of cancer in 2015 at the age of 44.

From the Junior Canadiens, Pietrangelo was taken third overall by the Mississauga IceDogs in the 2006 Ontario Hockey League draft, two spots after Steven

Stamkos. After Pietrangelo put up 105 points over two OHL seasons, the latter after the team moved to Niagara, the St. Louis Blues took him fourth overall in the 2008 NHL Entry Draft.

The Blues pondered keeping the 18-year-old for 2008–09, but he was sent back down to the OHL, where he captained the IceDogs. That season he won a gold medal with Team Canada at the 2009 World Junior Championship, and then a year later he had 12 points in six World Junior games and was named the tournament's best defenseman while winning silver.

In his first full NHL season, in 2010–11, the 6-foot-3, 205-pound defenseman showed he belonged permanently. He led all Blues defensemen in points (43), plus-minus (plus-18) and shots (161). Then at the 2011 World Championship he had five points in seven games and was voted the top defenseman.

The following season Pietrangelo led all NHL blue-liners with six game-winning goals, and his 51 points were fifth among defensemen. At 22 he became the youngest defenseman in franchise history to have consecutive seasons of 40 or more points, and a few years later he became the first with at least 40 points in each of his first four full NHL seasons, a total he's reached in seven of his eight full seasons. Since 2010–11 he's ninth among NHL defensemen in goals (92) and points (395) and seventh in average ice time (24:53).

In 2016 the Blues went to the Western Conference Final for the first time in 15 years, and Pietrangelo's 28:48 minutes of ice time per game in the playoffs were the most by any Blues defenseman over more than one round since Al MacInnis and Chris Pronger in 2001. In the off-season he was named the captain of a team on the rise.

"It makes me excited to know I could be the first captain to raise the Stanley Cup in the city of St. Louis," said Pietrangelo.

After a second-round loss to the Nashville Predators in the 2017 playoffs, Pietrangelo set career highs in goals (15), assists (39) and points (54) in 2017–18, but it was all for naught. The Blues failed to make the playoffs, prompting a roster overhaul.

It didn't start well. The Blues were at the bottom of the standings in early January 2019 before they caught fire. Under new coach Craig Berube they were the NHL's hottest team in the second half, and they rode that momentum and Pietrangelo's leadership all the way to the Stanley Cup Final against the Boston Bruins.

In Game 7 Pietrangelo led the way again. His assist on Ryan O'Reilly's opening goal set a franchise record for assists in the playoffs (16), and his goal with eight seconds left in the first period stood as the Cup winner. He finished the postseason tops among all defensemen in scoring with 19 points.

Pietrangelo fulfilled his dream when commissioner Gary Bettman handed him the Stanley Cup — the Blues' first since entering the NHL in 1967. He hoisted it high with the help of those around his wrist and in his heart. They'd been with him all along.

Won gold at the 2009 World Junior Championship
Won gold at the 2014 Olympics
Won the World Cup of Hockey in 2016
Played in the 2018 NHL All-Star Game
Won the Stanley Cup in 2019

P.K. SUBBAN

TRADED
New Jersey Devils
on June 22, 2019

After the Canadiens traded P.K. Subban, a season ticket holder took out a full-page ad in the *Montreal Gazette* to thank him for his service to the team and city. "You are an amazing and influential role model for my children and I am going to miss not having you as a Montreal Canadien," read the open letter from Dr. Charles Kowalski.

Such is the love that Montreal has for one of its favorite sons, the heir to the Flying Frenchman and the most entertaining man in a hidebound sport.

Subban wore the Bleu, Blanc et Rouge with obvious pride and made a $10 million donation to Montreal Children's Hospital, a record for a Canadian athlete. Together with Carey Price he was going to bring the glory back to Les Glorieux.

Until June 29, 2016, when the Canadiens shocked the hockey world by sending Subban to the Nashville Predators for Shea Weber. Montreal general manager Marc Bergevin claimed it was simply an opportunity to upgrade his team, while nebulous stories emerged of discord in the dressing room and a clash with then-coach Michel Therrien.

Subban can be thrilling on the ice, but it's a high-risk, high-reward proposition that doesn't sit well with some coaches, including Mike Babcock, coach of Canada's Olympic teams in 2010 and 2014 and its World Cup of Hockey team in 2016. It's the reason that Subban saw very little ice time in Sochi and why he was left off the roster entirely at the World Cup.

Pernell Karl Subban was born and raised in Rexdale,

a diverse neighborhood in northwest Toronto, and his father, Karl, used to take him downtown for late-night skates in front of Toronto City Hall.

P.K. is one of five children and the oldest of three sons, all of whom were drafted in the NHL after graduating from the Ontario Hockey League's Belleville Bulls. Over four years he became the franchise's highest scoring defenseman and won gold medals with Canada at the World Juniors in 2008 and 2009.

After being drafted by the Canadiens 43rd overall in 2007, Subban stormed into the league in the 2010 playoffs and won the Norris Trophy three years later, just a month after turning 24.

The 2014 playoffs were Subban's signature Montreal moment. He had four goals and three assists in a seven-game series against the reviled Boston Bruins, including a tide-turning breakaway goal. Before Game 7 in Boston he said, "I can't wait for the crowd, the noise, the energy in the building. I can't wait to take that away from them."

Many expected Subban to be named captain in 2015, but the team voted for Max Pacioretty. Less than a year later Subban was a Predator.

Subban brought his thunderous hip-checks, cannonading slap shots and sartorial splendor to Nashville. By the end of the year he'd led the Predators to their first Stanley Cup Final in franchise history, where they faced and fell to the Pittsburgh Penguins.

Subban was limited to 63 games in 2018–19 because of an upper-body injury and had just nine goals and 31 points. He didn't spend a lot of time out of the spotlight, however; his social media romance with American skier Lindsey Vonn, a multiple Olympic gold medalist, saw to that.

He also used social media as a force for good. After hearing about a young hockey player in Michigan who had endured racial abuse on the ice, Subban posted an inspirational message for 13-year-old Ty Cornett. The video went viral and affirmed the Cornett family's decision to keep Ty in hockey.

After the Predators fell in the first round of the 2019 playoffs a change was needed, and general manager David Poile has shown he's not afraid to pull the trigger. With a surplus of defensemen and goals at a premium, he traded Subban to the New Jersey Devils to free up salary cap space to sign forward Matt Duchene.

The Predators' highest-paid player was also its most vocal so there were whispers about other contributing factors. It will always be a part of the Subban conversation, based on his much-needed originality, his over-sized personality and hockey's old-school mentality.

Subban came by his advice to Cornett honestly, and it will continue to serve Subban well as he enters the next phase of his career:

"As long as you're still breathing in this world, you've got to believe in yourself and let nobody tell you what you can and can't do, especially if it's because of the color of your skin," Subban said in the video. "All we have to do is understand ourself, believe in ourself and keep trying and keep pushing forward. So I just want to tell you that when you're playing hockey, you play because you love the game and you want to play. Let nobody take that away from you."

Won gold at the 2008 and 2009 World Junior Championship

Won the Norris Trophy in 2013

Won gold at the 2014 Olympics

Played in three NHL All-Star Games (2016, 2017, 2018)

BEN BISHOP

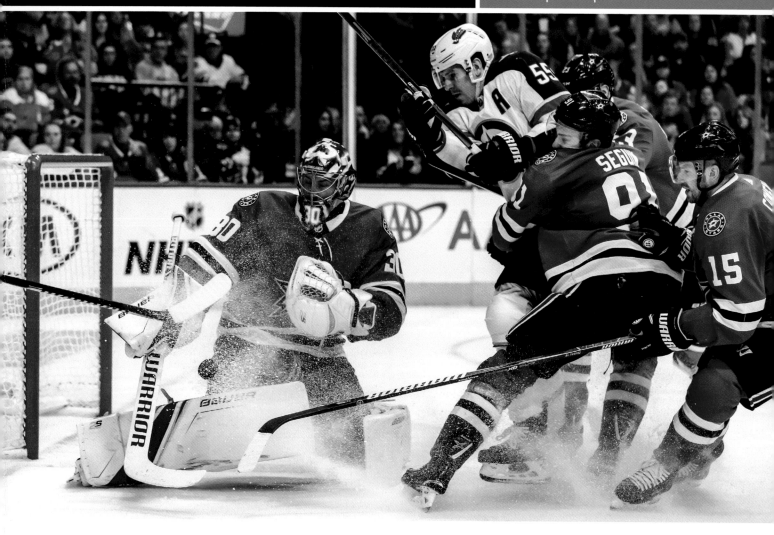

In early 2017 the Tampa Bay Lightning had almost 13 feet of elite goaltending and had to make a decision. They went with the short one.

Andrei Vasilevskiy, a first-round draft pick and an emerging star under contract, was eight years younger than 6-foot-7 Ben Bishop. With Bishop approaching free agency they put their faith in the 6-foot-4 Vasilevskiy.

Bishop was dealt to the LA Kings at the 2017 trade deadline but played only seven games before they traded him to the Dallas Stars for a fourth-round draft pick less than three months later instead of losing him to free agency. Three days later he signed a six-year, $29.5 million contract with the Stars, who were 29th in the NHL in goals allowed per game (3.17) and last in save percentage (.893) in 2016–17.

It was a homecoming of sorts, after his first one didn't work out.

Born in Denver but raised in St. Louis, Bishop was a diehard Blues fan growing up and played for the Junior Blues until he was 17, when he left to play for the Texas Tornado of the North American Hockey League.

Bishop had already qualified for college admission at that point, which was his parents' prerequisite for him decamping to Texas, and he started at the University of Maine months after the Blues drafted him in the third round, 85th overall, in 2005.

He signed his first professional contract as a college junior and promised his parents he'd finish his degree, which he did just one semester later than he would have if he'd stayed, studying on the long American Hockey League bus rides to keep up.

The happy hometown ending didn't quite work out in St. Louis. After three seasons at Maine, Bishop played just 13 games with the Blues between 2008 and 2011. He spent most of his time with the AHL's Peoria Rivermen before being traded to the Ottawa Senators in 2011.

Bishop only got into 23 games with Ottawa from 2011 to 2013 before he was traded to the Lightning, where he finally got the chance to play regularly. In 2013–14, his first full season in Tampa Bay, he had a 37-14-7 record, a 2.23 goals-against average and a .924 save percentage, and he finished third in Vezina Trophy voting.

The following season Bishop had a career-high 40 wins, and in the 2015 playoffs he faced off against the Presidents' Trophy–winning New York Rangers and goaltending legend Henrik Lundqvist at Madison Square Garden in Game 7 of the Eastern Conference Final. Lundqvist had won all six of his Game 7s and the Rangers had never lost in Game 7 at home in franchise history.

Bishop shut them out and the 2–0 win sent the Lightning to the 2015 Stanley Cup Final. They lost to the Chicago Blackhawks in six games, and less than two years later Bishop was gone.

The trade that eventually ended up with Bishop in Dallas turned out to be a win/win for both the Stars and Lightning; he and Vasilevskiy were two of the three finalists for the 2019 Vezina Trophy.

In 2018–19, Bishop set new career highs and finished top 3 in save percentage (.934), goals-against average (1.98) and shutouts (seven). His save percentage led the NHL and set a franchise record, and it was the ninth-best in NHL history.

Most importantly, Bishop got the Stars back to the postseason in the home stretch. He was 8-1-0 with a 0.78 goals-against average and .972 save percentage in his last 10 games, and 11-3-0 with a 1.15 goals-against average, .962 save percentage and six shutouts over his final 15. That included a shutout streak of 233:04 minutes from March 2 to 19, the longest in the NHL since 2015–16.

Bishop led Dallas to a first-round upset over the division-winning Nashville Predators. But the Stars lost 2–1 in double overtime in Game 7 in the second round to the team that drafted him in the city he grew up in, despite his career-high 52 saves.

Maybe Blues fans' chanting his name in an attempt to rattle him was actually a tribute to a local boy who almost eliminated their team all by himself, or one of life's full-circle moments.

For his family in the stands, including infant son Benjamin Bishop IV, it was just nice to see him as an established star in a crease in St. Louis.

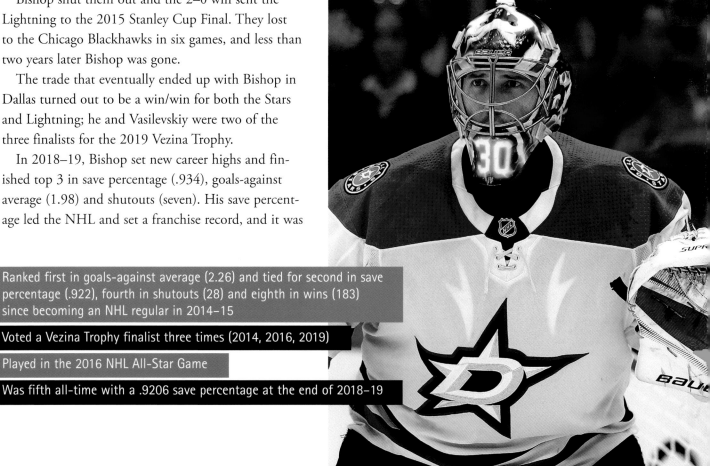

Ranked first in goals-against average (2.26) and tied for second in save percentage (.922), fourth in shutouts (28) and eighth in wins (183) since becoming an NHL regular in 2014–15

Voted a Vezina Trophy finalist three times (2014, 2016, 2019)

Played in the 2016 NHL All-Star Game

Was fifth all-time with a .9206 save percentage at the end of 2018–19

PATRIK LAINE

CENTRAL DIVISION | Jets | Right Wing

seven goals to share the tournament lead with Matthews. In the Finnish Elite League, Laine was first among rookies with 17 goals and 33 points in 46 games, and he led Tappara to the 2016 Finnish League championship, scoring 10 goals in 18 games to win the Jari Kurri Award as playoff MVP.

A couple weeks later Laine went to the World Championship. A boy among men — albeit a 6-foot-5, 206-pound one — he tied for the tournament lead with seven goals and was named MVP as Finland won silver.

That kind of success would normally make Laine an easy choice for number one pick. Fortunately for the Jets, 2016 was not most years. Though they lost the lottery, Winnipeg was going back to the future. The first version of the team, before it moved to Arizona, had Teemu Selanne arrive from Finland and shatter the NHL rookie record with 76 goals in 1992–93. The second iteration of the Jets, formerly the Atlanta Thrashers, now had themselves a similarly electrifying Finn.

In the first eight games of his NHL career, Laine had six goals (including a hat trick), one of which featured a goal celebration that nodded to his countryman, mimicking Selanne's stick twirl before placing it back in its (imaginary) scabbard on his hip.

With his rocket of a shot and exuberant goal celebrations, Laine also brought to mind a young Alex Ovechkin — perhaps the most apt comparison for both him and Matthews.

Laine is an explosive winger, capable of blowing the puck through goaltenders, while Matthews is a more subtly skilled centerman, like Sidney Crosby. Their rivalry is also similar to Crosby and Ovechkin's, based more on proximity in age and talent and media encouragement than any real personal animosity.

Although the Jets missed the playoffs, their golden child finished 2016–17 with 36 goals and 64 points,

For Canada, 2016 was an annus horribilis. Not one Canadian team qualified for the postseason, so the most dramatic hockey coverage was the draft lottery. Five of the top six draft picks went to Canadian teams, with the Toronto Maple Leafs taking Arizona's Auston Matthews first and the Winnipeg Jets choosing Patrik Laine of Tampere, Finland, next.

Laine, for one, believed he should've been first: "I know that's how good I am, and I can say that. It's not a problem for me. And if that's a problem to somebody else, it's not my problem."

He's not wrong. Laine had already proven himself before the draft with a season for the ages.

It began with Finland winning the 2016 World Junior gold medal on home ice, with Laine scoring

second to Matthews in both categories and Calder voting. Laine finished seventh in the NHL in goals, tied for sixth in even-strength goals (27) and fourth in goals per game (0.49), and played in his first All-Star Game.

"I look back and, if I was the same age, there's no way that I'd be that ready right away," said Selanne, who was 22 when he reached the NHL. "I'm so proud of how he's played and how he's handled himself in his first season. It's unbelievable."

There was no sophomore slump either. In 2017–18 the 19-year-old set two franchise records with a 15-game point streak that included at least one goal in six straight games. Over that span, in which the Jets went 10-4-1, he had 18 goals and eight assists.

And for the second straight year he was a runner-up for a major individual award, this time to Ovechkin for the Maurice Richard Trophy. Laine's 44 goals were second to Ovechkin's 49, he scored in 37 games, 11 more than his rookie year, and he led the NHL in power-play goals with 20.

The first real adversity of Laine's charmed career came in season three. After scoring 18 goals in November 2018, including a hat trick at home in

Helsinki, he went 15 games without a goal in January and February, registering only four assists in that time. He admitted the slump robbed him of confidence and the joy of playing. Laine still finished with 30 goals in 2018–19. He has 110 for his career, just one behind Matthews, and he only turned 21 during the playoffs.

When it was done Laine put it in perspective: "Point and goal wise, I had a better season last year, but I would say I was a way better player all around this year than I was when the season ended last year."

Even Selanne came down from his rookie high — his second highest season total was 52 goals — but the Jets will take a slump or two if it helps Laine grow into Teemu 2.0.

Won gold at the 2016 World Junior Championship	
Won the Finnish Elite League championship and named playoff MVP in 2016	
Won silver at the 2016 World Championship and named MVP	
Second in Calder Trophy voting in 2017	
Runner-up for the Maurice Richard Trophy in 2018	

MIKKO RANTANEN

CENTRAL DIVISION | Avalanche | Right Wing

Mikko Rantanen is the first NHL player from Nousiainen, a small town in the southwest of Finland. It might be why he flew under the radar, even in that hockey-mad country.

At 16, the 5-foot-10, 175-pound Rantanen joined TPS Turku in the Liiga, Finland's top flight. Two years and six inches of height later, the 18-year-old was named an alternate captain and was second on the team in scoring with 28 points in 56 games, tops in the league for players under 20, while averaging only 16:14 of ice time. He also won the Ville Peltonen Award as the league's playoff MVP.

Rantanen wasn't a marquee name in the 2015 draft class, which gave the NHL Connor McDavid and Jack Eichel, but the 10th overall pick by the Colorado Avalanche made the team out of training camp. He played nine games at the start of the 2015–16 season before being sent down to the American Hockey League's San Antonio Rampage. There he had 24 goals and 60 points in 52 games and was named AHL co-rookie of the year.

Taking a midseason break, Rantanen returned home to play in the 2016 World Juniors. He scored a goal against the Russians in the final as the Finns won gold on home soil, but even as captain he didn't receive the same coverage as teammates Patrik Laine, Sebastian Aho and Jesse Puljujarvi.

Rantanen finished the season with a silver at the World Championship and started the next in Colorado. His growth spurt meant he was still a bit "clumsy," according to line-mate Nathan MacKinnon, when he entered the NHL. But in 2017–18, his second full season, he finished second on the team to MacKinnon and tied for 16th in the NHL with 84 points — the most by a Finnish-born player since Teemu Selanne had 94 and Olli Jokinen had 91 in 2006–07.

The following season Rantanen came out blazing. He had 16 assists and 21 points in 12 games in October 2018 to be named the NHL's player of the month. He was the first player to reach the 30-, 40- and 50-point marks, and he hit 60 points just a few hours after Art Ross and Hart Trophy winner Nikita Kucherov on December 27.

Rantanen tied for or led the NHL in scoring for 66 straight days from October 23 to December 27 and was the second Avalanche player to have the lead at Christmas, after Hall of Famer Peter Forsberg. His 59 points were the most by anyone at the holiday break since Sidney Crosby had 60 in 2010–11. During the 2018 calendar year, Rantanen had the second-most points (113) of any player, behind Connor McDavid (121), and his 79 assists led the NHL.

"Are we tip of the iceberg-ing this and we don't even know what's going to happen?'" asked Avalanche television analyst Peter McNab. "Because if he is steps away from getting to where he is ultimately going to get, it's almost close to unstoppable. Unless you go back to the '70s or '80s and just beat the heck out of him.

"The game is sort of at that spot with his abilities where he may dominate, I mean, truly dominate, he and MacKinnon for a long time."

Still just 22, Rantanen cooled off a little in the second half and missed the last eight games of the regular season with an upper-body injury. He finished with 87 points in 74 games and led the club with 16 power-play goals, tied for sixth in the NHL and the most by an Avalanche player since Joe Sakic had 16 in 2006–07. In the playoffs he added six goals and 14 points in 12 games.

Now 6-foot-4 and 215 pounds, Rantanen could play the physical game, but he's still the skinny kid who learned to play with vision and a high hockey IQ.

"His hands are top notch," according to Blues defenseman Joel Edmundson. And his slick mitts aren't the only things that endear him to teammates.

"He's an easy guy to be around. He treats everybody well. He's a good teammate. He knows how to have fun here at the rink and make it fun for everyone else. And he also knows how to work," said Avalanche captain Gabriel Landeskog, who makes up the third member of the MGM line along with Rantanen and MacKinnon, one of the league's most exciting trios.

"I don't know any grumpy Finns or Swedes," replied Rantanen.

Captained Finland to gold at the 2016 World Junior Championship	
Shared the 2016 Dudley "Red" Garret Memorial Trophy as AHL rookie of the year	
Won silver at the 2016 World Championship	
Played in the 2019 NHL All-Star Game	

VLADIMIR TARASENKO

CENTRAL DIVISION | Blues | Right Wing

Vladimir Tarasenko scored on the first two shots of his NHL career. His grandfather was probably disappointed he didn't get the hat trick.

The goals came on January 19, 2013, against Jimmy Howard and the Detroit Red Wings, the former team of his idol Sergei Fedorov and one of the reasons Tarasenko wears No. 91. It's also the year of his birth, in Novosibirsk, Siberia.

Tarasenko spent much of his youth there being raised by his grandfather and namesake while his father, Andrei, was pursuing his own hockey dreams.

The elder Vladimir was the director of a soccer academy, but his grandson wanted to follow in his father's skates. The young man was groomed to succeed with a little tough love. "When [Vladimir] had a fever my wife would still dress him warmly and take him for a walk outside in winter. This was how we hardened him," recalled his grandfather fondly.

Tarasenko made HC Sibir Novosibirsk's second team when he was 14, scoring seven goals in one game that season. The next preseason he earned a tryout with the first team, which was coached by his father.

If there were any questions of nepotism, Tarasenko answered them by scoring a goal the first time he touched the puck in the Kontinental Hockey League.

But it wasn't always smooth sailing for father and son. "They were always punching each other, screaming at each other," said Jori Lehtera, Tarasenko's ex-teammate with the St. Louis Blues and Novosibirsk. "They had more like a coach-player relationship."

Tarasenko eventually left his hometown to play for SKA St. Petersburg, where he was named captain at the age of 18, and after he represented Russia at the 2010 World Junior Championship the Blues traded David Rundblad to Ottawa for the opportunity to draft him 16th overall.

In 2011 Tarasenko returned to the World Juniors as Team Russia's captain. He left the gold medal game with a rib injury in the second period but came back for the third when Russia trailed Canada 3–0. The captain spearheaded the comeback with the game-tying goal and an assist on the go-ahead goal in a 5–3 win.

By 2014–15 Tarasenko had established himself as an NHL star. He led the Blues with 37 goals, the start of five straight seasons of at least 33. He's third in the NHL in that span with 182 goals, trailing leader Alex Ovechkin and just one goal behind John Tavares.

In 2015 the Blues rewarded Tarasenko with an eight-year contract averaging $7.5 million per season, the highest in franchise history. In 2015–16 he led the Blues in regular-season (40) and playoff goals (nine) as they reached the Western Conference Final.

After coming within two wins of the Stanley Cup Final, hopes and expectations were high in St. Louis for the 2016–17 season. The team underachieved, but the Blues' lone representative at the All-Star Game gave one young fan the birthday of a lifetime.

At the Blues' Hockey Fights Cancer event in 2015 Tarasenko met Arianna Dougan, who was fighting neuroblastoma. In 2017 he brought her with the Blues on their charter plane to Arizona and Colorado for her 11th birthday. Arianna died later that year, but her memory was alive and inspirational in 2019. Tarasenko was coming back from reconstructive shoulder surgery in the off-season and the Blues were last overall on January 3. But the team steadily rose up the standings in the second half and then stormed through the playoffs, in large part because of Tarasenko's improved play at both ends of the rink.

Tarasenko contributed 11 goals and had an eight-game point streak in the playoffs as the Blues beat the Boston Bruins in seven games to capture the first Stanley Cup in franchise history.

Tarasenko shared the win with his family — his wife posted a picture of him cradling the Cup in one arm and their newborn child in the other — but there were others who helped along the way. The night the Blues advanced to the franchise's first Stanley Cup Final since 1970 he sent a text to Lori Zucker, Arianna's mom. It simply said, "She is in my heart."

Without her the championship was "bittersweet," said Zucker, but "[Tarasenko] will always, always, always be in my heart."

| Won gold at the 2011 World Junior Championship |
| Played in three NHL All-Star Games (2015, 2016, 2017) |
| Featured on the cover of EA Sports' *NHL 17* |
| Won the Stanley Cup in 2019 |

DUSTIN BYFUGLIEN

CENTRAL DIVISION | Jets | Defense

grades weren't up to standard so he just practiced with the team. "I was like, 'Whatever, I'll just go do something different. I'll go fishing, I'll go snowmobiling,'" recalled Byfuglien.

Word spread about the linebacker in skates anyway, and the Chicago Mission midget team invited Byfuglien to join them. "I think that's when I realized that, alright, I can actually, probably, maybe, do something, a little bit, with this hockey stuff," he said.

Byfuglien was taken by the Brandon Wheat Kings in the seventh round of the 2001 Western Hockey League draft then was later traded to the Prince George Cougars. In 2002–03, his NHL draft season, he had 39 points in 56 games, nine more points than fellow WHL defenseman Dion Phaneuf in 15 fewer games.

While Phaneuf was selected ninth overall in 2003, Byfuglien had to wait until the eighth round, 245th overall, for the Chicago Blackhawks to call his name. Not that he was aware of it. The Blackhawks couldn't reach him after the draft and finally had to show up at the family home to inform him. "Normally when they get that call, it's the happiest day, the biggest day in a kid's life," recounted general manager Stan Bowman. "Buff didn't even know he'd been drafted."

Byfuglien's first full season was in 2007–08, which included a move from defense to forward. He's switched back and forth throughout his career when the need has arisen, evidence of his underrated skating ability and high hockey IQ.

Byfuglien spent most of the 2009–10 season on defense, but moved up to forward for the playoffs. He tied for the team lead with 11 playoff goals, including a hat trick in the second round against the Vancouver Canucks, three game-winners in a sweep of the San Jose Sharks in the Western Conference Final, a two-goal, four-point night in Game 5 of the Stanley Cup

Whether he's filling out a uniform or a stat sheet, Big Buff is hard to miss. Officially listed at 6-foot-5 and 260 pounds, give or take a little on the weight, Dustin Byfuglien is a wrecking ball. But it's not just hits and penalty minutes. He's also racking up ice time, shots, goals and assists. Not that he's checking out the box scores the next day. Sports, according to Byfuglien, "aren't my cup of tea."

That might be the reason for Byfuglien's laissez-faire attitude toward hockey growing up, and even after his name was called at the NHL Entry Draft.

Byfuglien spent his childhood in Roseau, Minnesota, living in a trailer with his mother in her parents' yard. He was good enough to make the Roseau Rams, winners of seven state high school championships, but his

Final against the Philadelphia Flyers and a goal in the Game 6 win that clinched the Cup.

That was his swansong in Chicago, however. Hard against the salary cap, the Blackhawks traded him to Atlanta during the summer.

Playing defense for the Thrashers in 2010–11, Byfuglien's 20 goals and 53 points ranked first and fourth among all NHL defensemen, and he played in his first of four All-Star Games. For the 2011–12 season, after one year in Atlanta, he relocated with the team to Winnipeg.

Now an elder statesman on an elite team, Byfuglien sets an example with his energy and effort. He led the

league in average ice time in 2016–17 (27:26), and among defensemen he was fifth in points (52) and second in shots (241) and penalty minutes (117).

Byfuglien was first on the Jets in ice time in 2017–18 (24:20), and he upped it to 26:30 in the playoffs while scoring 16 points in 17 games as the Jets made a run to the Western Conference Final.

In 2018–19 Byfuglien led the team in ice time (24:22) for the fourth straight year, even after suffering a concussion and playing through leg and ankle injuries that cost him nearly half the season. That didn't stop him from also leading the team in penalty minutes (69) for the fifth consecutive season.

A unique mix of toughness and talent Byfuglien is seventh in penalty minutes among active players and also in scoring among defensemen since entering the league.

"He is intimidating," said teammate Matt Hendricks. "He is kind of the X-Factor. I don't think there is anyone like him in the game."

Won the Stanley Cup in 2010

Played in four NHL All-Star Games (2011, 2012, 2015, 2016)

Played for Team USA at the 2016 World Cup of Hockey

Led the NHL in average ice time in 2016–17 (27:26)

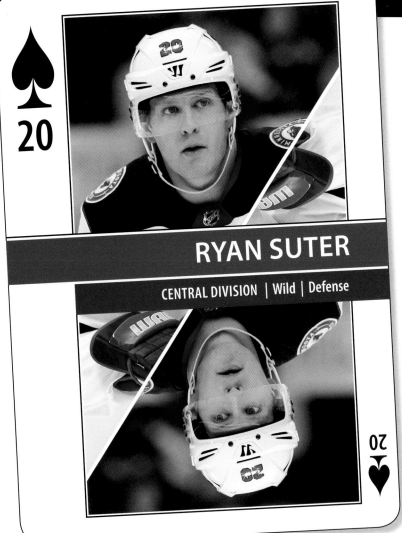

20 ♠

RYAN SUTER

CENTRAL DIVISION | Wild | Defense

Ryan Suter is almost more impressive for what he doesn't do. On the ice he doesn't waste energy and rarely takes penalties; off the ice he doesn't like to draw attention to himself or his philanthropy, and he's careful with the money he's earned as a strong, silent, skilled defenseman.

Suter plays with a simplicity that's only possible because he's an intelligent player who can control the pace of the game. It also allows him to munch minutes — he's been the NHL leader in ice time four times.

The simplicity extends to his ride. Suter bought himself a Ford SUV with his rookie contract and drove it for 11 years, until his wife encouraged him to upgrade to a Cadillac Escalade. "I feel guilty driving that car," said Suter, "because my dad never had that."

Suter wears number 20 as a tribute to his father, Bob, who was a member of the 1980 U.S. Olympic hockey team that upset the Soviet Union in the Miracle on Ice. Bob was drafted by the Los Angeles Kings but never played in the NHL. After his minor-league career ended he opened a sporting goods store and ran the Madison Capitols youth hockey organization that Ryan's grandfather co-founded.

After Ryan was drafted by the Nashville Predators seventh overall in 2003 Bob would drive nine hours to watch his son play and then drive right back after the game to open Bob Suter's Capitol Ice Arena in Middleton, Wisconsin. He died of a heart attack there in 2014.

Ryan's younger brother now runs the arena and coaches the under-18 team, and his mother works in hockey administration. In the off-season Ryan practices with the kids and helps with arena renovations. "They're hockey royalty here," said Tom Garrity, manager of the Tier 1 Capitols.

Suter joined the Predators in 2005–06, and the following year he was paired with fellow 2003 draftee Shea Weber. Over the next six seasons they were arguably the best blue line tandem in the NHL.

The pair broke up in 2012, when the free agent chose Minnesota. There he signed a 13-year, $98 million free agent contract with the Wild, as did Zach Parise, one of Suter's best friends and a teammate on the U.S. team that won silver at the 2010 Olympics.

Leaving Nashville was difficult, but Suter's wife grew up in the Twin Cities and Minnesota was the closest team to his family.

In his first season with the Wild, Suter was a first-team All-Star and the runner-up for the Norris Trophy after averaging 27:17 minutes a game. The following season he averaged 29:25 minutes a game, which was 2:21 more than anyone else in the league. He was the

first player since Nicklas Lidstrom in 2002–03 to surpass the 29-minute mark.

A believer in rolling six defensemen, new coach Bruce Boudreau limited his minutes in 2016–17, but Suter still tied for the league lead with a plus-34 rating, playing all 82 games with only 36 penalty minutes.

Suter, who had missed just five games with the Wild, had tied a career high in points with 51 when he suffered a career-threatening break of his right fibula and the talus in his ankle with four games left in the 2017–18 season. Three screws were put in his

ankle by a foot specialist who had just worked with Weber, and the former partners spent time comparing and commiserating.

Suter couldn't put any weight on his ankle for three months, which forced him to hire someone to repair the arena at home and made him question whether he'd even be able to walk again.

Off-season rehab started with seniors' aquafit but got Suter back in time for training camp, and he defied logic and expectations by leading the NHL in ice time once again in 2018–19, playing all 82 games and averaging 26:42. He has now played over 27,000 minutes (450 hours) in his career — more than anyone else in the NHL since he entered the league.

He'd earned a rest, but Suter joined Team USA for the World Championship after the Wild missed the playoffs for the first time since he joined the team, ankle be damned.

Taking time off is about the only thing Suter doesn't do well.

| Won gold at the 2004 World Junior Championship |
| Won silver at the 2010 Olympics |
| Played in three NHL All-Star Games (2012, 2015, 2017) |
| Led the NHL in average ice time four times (2012–13, 2013–14, 2014–15, 2018–19) |
| Tied for the NHL lead in plus-minus (+34) in 2016–17 |

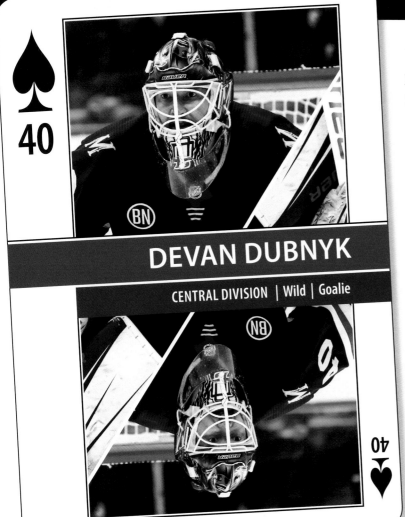

DEVAN DUBNYK

CENTRAL DIVISION | Wild | Goalie

Falcons before sticking with the Oilers in 2010–11.

"As a young player you have no idea what it's going to take. And that's probably a good thing, because it's pretty daunting," said Dubnyk. "I was called up 11 times, up and down, from Springfield. Like all young goalies, I thought I could get [to the NHL] fast, but it's really so rare."

Between 2010 and 2013 Dubnyk had a .917 save percentage and 2.58 goals-against average. However, over 32 games in the final year of his contract in 2013–14, his goals-against average ballooned to 3.36 while his save percentage dropped to .894.

Management shipped him to Nashville in January 2014, and in his only two games with the Predators, Dubnyk allowed nine goals. He was then traded to the Montreal Canadiens and played eight games the rest of the season, all with the AHL's Hamilton Bulldogs.

Dubnyk was miserable and a long way from his wife and their newborn son who were back in Edmonton. Even after Carey Price got hurt in the 2014 playoffs he was still third on the depth chart behind Dustin Tokarski and Peter Budaj, so Dubnyk asked to leave the team to be with his family.

Returning home was the reset he needed. He still believed he could play and the Arizona Coyotes agreed, signing him to a one-year, $800,000 deal. Both Dubnyk's technique and confidence improved under Arizona goalie coach Sean Burke, and as Mike Smith's backup he put up decent numbers in 19 games.

On January 15, 2015, exactly one year after Edmonton traded him, the desperate Minnesota Wild acquired Dubnyk. They were 18-19-5 and eight points out of a playoff spot. "To be as honest as possible, we were just trying to get a save," according to the Wild's general manager at the time, Chuck Fletcher.

What a difference a year makes. In 12 months Devan Dubnyk went from languishing in the American Hockey League and asking to be released to being a Vezina Trophy finalist.

In 2004 the Regina, Saskatchewan, native was named the Canadian Hockey League's Scholastic Player of the Year and was taken 14th overall by the Edmonton Oilers in the entry draft. Calm, funny and smart, the 6-foot-6 Dubnyk had the necessary qualities for success in an NHL crease. He would need them all to take the slings and arrows of the profession.

After the draft Dubnyk spent two more seasons in junior with the Kamloops Blazers, a year with the Stockton Thunder in the East Coast Hockey League and over two seasons with the AHL's Springfield

"We were losing a lot of games, and our season was right on the brink of getting away from us. We got very lucky. Good fortune smiled warmly upon us."

Dubnyk shut out the Buffalo Sabres and started the next 38 games. With their new goalie in net the Wild went an incredible 27-9-2, with Dubnyk posting a 1.72 goals-against average and a .936 save percentage. He was a finalist for the Vezina Trophy, finished fourth in voting for the Hart and won the 2015 Masterton Trophy for perseverance, sportsmanship and dedication to hockey. He also earned job security with a six-year, $26 million contract.

In the four seasons that followed Dubnyk was a Wild workhorse. He averaged almost 65 games played and 35 wins a year, while posting a 2.41 goals-against average and a .918 save percentage in that span. He was first in the NHL in total saves (6,718), tied for second in wins (138) and tied for fourth in goals-against average.

In 2018–19 he led all goaltenders in the league with 67 games played and was fifth in saves (1,714), earning him his third trip to the All-Star Game. It's a game the 33-year-old could've been forgiven for skipping, considering his workload, but he wasn't going to miss out.

"After going through the stuff that I did before I came to Minnesota, I've always said to myself, 'I'm going to make sure to be grateful for every opportunity I get,'" said Dubnyk, who enjoyed the weekend with Jennifer and their sons, Nate and Parker. "This is another part of the story. It's something special that I'm just never going to turn down. I've been right at the bottom, so I'm not about to start turning away recognition at the top."

Named WHL and CHL Scholastic Player of the Year in 2004

Won gold at the 2006 World Junior Championship

Awarded the Bill Masterton Trophy in 2015

Played in three NHL All-Star Games (2016, 2017, 2019)

Finished first among goalies in games played (67) in 2018–19

PACICIC DIVISION

FIRST TEAM

122	**JOHNNY GAUDREAU**	Flames	Left Wing
124	**ANZE KOPITAR**	Kings	Center
126	**CONNOR McDAVID**	Oilers	Center
128	**BRENT BURNS**	Sharks	Defense
130	**MARK GIORDANO**	Flames	Defense
132	**MARC-ANDRÉ FLEURY**	Golden Knights	Goalie

SECOND TEAM

134	**LEON DRAISAITL**	Oilers	Center
136	**JOE PAVELSKI**	Sharks	Center
138	**ELIAS PETTERSSON**	Canucks	Center
140	**DREW DOUGHTY**	Kings	Defense
142	**ERIK KARLSSON**	Sharks	Defense
144	**MARTIN JONES**	Sharks	Goalie

BLACK ACES

146	**BROCK BOESER**	Canucks	Right Wing
148	**SEAN MONAHAN**	Flames	Center
150	**MARK STONE**	Golden Knights	Right Wing
152	**OLIVER EKMAN-LARSSON**	Coyotes	Defense
154	**SHEA THEODORE**	Golden Knights	Defense
156	**JOHN GIBSON**	Ducks	Goalie

JOHNNY GAUDREAU

Johnny Hockey's nickname began as a play on Johnny Football's. It invokes the youthful exuberance that both Johnnys displayed while tearing up the collegiate ranks in their respective sports. While Texas A&M quarterback Johnny Manziel's immaturity landed him more on *TMZ* than *Monday Night Football* and he's now out of the game, Johnny Gaudreau is a legitimate NHL star, even if he still looks like a kid.

The native of Salem, New Jersey, was a child prodigy, skating rings around older kids. When Jane Gaudreau suggested to her husband, Guy, that Johnny might be in the NHL some day, Guy tempered expectations: "Whoa, you sound like some of my crazy hockey parents. He's not going to the NHL."

Guy knew what he was talking about. A member of the athletic hall of fame at Norwich University in Vermont, he was hockey director at Hollydell Ice Arena, where Johnny learned to skate.

Still dominating while at Gloucester Catholic High School, Gaudreau joined the Dubuque Fighting Saints of the United States Hockey League in 2010–11. The 17-year-old scored 72 points in 60 games and earned Rookie of the Year honors.

That convinced the Calgary Flames, who drafted Gaudreau in the fourth round in 2011, 104th overall, well ahead of Central Scouting's projection of 193rd overall. With Gaudreau clocking in at 5-foot-6 and 137 pounds, even that projection was generous for a winger of his size.

Gaudreau chose to hone his game (and grow) at Boston College, winning the NCAA title in his freshman year after being cut from USA Hockey's 2012

World Junior team. "He takes those setbacks, uses them to motivate him more and it has furthered his determination," said former Boston College associate head coach Greg Brown about the USA Hockey snub. "He is an incredibly competitive kid. Every day in practice, every little small game we play, you can see the fire come out in him." Gaudreau made the World Junior team in 2013 and led the tournament with seven goals en route to the U.S. winning gold.

A Hobey Baker finalist as a sophomore, Gaudreau stuck around Boston College to play another year with younger brother Matt in 2013–14. He won the national player of the year award as a junior and the next day signed with Calgary. The Flames welcomed him in style, flying him out by private jet to their last game of the 2013–14 season.

Gaudreau, who munched on Skittles during the flight, repaid them with a goal on his first NHL shot.

In his first full season Gaudreau was a finalist for the Calder Trophy after scoring 24 goals, leading all rookies in assists with 40 and tying for the rookie lead in points with 64. He also helped Calgary reach the playoffs for the first time in six years and led the team with nine points in 11 games. Gaudreau followed that up with 30 goals and 78 points in 2015–16, good for sixth in league scoring.

After four points in three games with Team North America at the 2016 World Cup of Hockey, Gaudreau skipped training camp over a contract impasse. He eventually signed a six-year, $40.5 million contract, and after a slow start he rebounded with 61 points and the Lady Byng Trophy, awarded for sportsmanship and gentlemanly conduct. He followed that up with 84 points in 2017–18.

In 2018–19 Gaudreau had career highs in goals (36), assists (63) and points (99), tying him for sev-enth in the NHL in points and ninth in assists.

The Professional Hockey Writers Association had Gaudreau as a midseason Hart Trophy finalist, but a nine-game goal drought dropped him down the list. He even busted out of that in style, however, recording a hat trick and six points in a 9–4 win over the New Jersey Devils.

Through his five full seasons Gaudreau has 387 points in 394 career games — only six players have more points in that span — and he's played in the All-Star Game every year, winning the puck control competition at the 2019 edition.

"When you watched him in college, you were always thinking, 'Can he do it in the NHL? Can he do it against the best players in the world?'" said Flames assistant general manager Craig Conroy, who accompanied Gaudreau to his first NHL game. "He's done everything that we could have hoped for — and more. He did all that stuff in college, but he just continues to get better. It's hard to imagine he could get better, but this year he's taken it to a whole new level again.

"It's special because when you're on that plane with him, these are all the things you were hoping for."

Won gold at the 2013 World Junior Championship

Won the Hobey Baker Award in 2014

Played in five NHL All-Star Games (2015, 2016, 2017, 2018, 2019)

Named to the NHL All-Rookie Team in 2015

Won the Lady Byng Trophy in 2017

ANZE KOPITAR

One of the most coveted assets in hockey is a big, offensively gifted yet defensively responsible center. To find such a unicorn, the Los Angeles Kings went all the way to Slovenia, a country with only 2 million people, seven rinks, and 158 men and 67 women over the age of 20 registered to play hockey.

Anze Kopitar, from Jesenice, a town in the northern part of the country near the Austrian border, is the first Slovene to play in the NHL. More common is his origin story. Playing on a backyard rink that his grandfather flooded, Anze spent hours out there pretending to be his dad, Matjaz, who was a national team player.

"He was always scoring big goals in big games, so I always wanted to be that guy, too," said Anze. "He was in the national championship, and I thought that was the best thing."

It was the biggest stage he could imagine as a boy, but when Slovenia hosted an international tournament, scouts who came to see players from the usual European hockey powers discovered a local product who could play. In 2004, at the age of 16, Kopitar left to play for Sodertalje SK in Sweden.

In 2005 Kopitar had 10 goals and 13 points for Slovenia in the B pool of the World Junior Championship, and 11 points in five games at the under-18 tournament. He also represented his country at the highest level for the first time in Olympic qualifying and at the World Championship, with his father as assistant coach.

It was the same year the Kings picked him 11th overall in the entry draft, and Kopitar made his NHL debut at 19 years old on October 6, 2006, scoring two goals against the Anaheim Ducks. In his second game he had three assists against the St. Louis Blues.

Kopitar led the Kings in scoring in 2007–08, the start of nine straight seasons that the center ranked first on the team. With 74 points in 2015–16 he broke Marcel Dionne's franchise record of eight consecutive years (1975–76 to 1982–83).

Kopitar's scoring exploits aren't limited to the regular season. He has 21 goals and 66 points in 79 career postseason games, including eight goals and 20 points in the 2012 playoffs, tied with then-captain Dustin Brown atop the NHL, to help lead the Kings to the franchise's first Stanley Cup.

In 2014 Wayne Gretzky, who knows something about playing in LA and being great, called Kopitar the third-best player in the world, behind Jonathan Toews and Sidney Crosby. In the playoffs Kopitar bettered them both, leading all players in assists (21) and points (26) as the Kings won their second championship.

Earlier in 2014 Slovenia defied all odds and logic by reaching the quarterfinals of the Sochi Olympics. At the helm was Matjaz Kopitar, who was cut from the Yugoslavian team just before the Sarajevo Olympics in 1984 but 30 years later fulfilled his Olympic dream as head coach of Slovenia. His son was the only NHL player on the Slovenian Olympic team.

The 2015–16 season was a banner one for Kopitar, who won the Frank J. Selke Trophy as best defensive forward and the Lady Byng Trophy for being the league's most sportsmanlike player. The Kings rewarded him with an eight-year, $80 million contract in 2016. In September of that year he captained Team Europe at the World Cup of Hockey. It was the sec-ond team that named him captain that summer after the Kings took the C off Brown's jersey and gave it to Kopitar, who had been Brown's lieutenant and alternate for eight seasons.

Fatigue from the World Cup and Olympic qualifying coupled with an arm injury led to a down year for Kopitar in 2016–17, but he bounced back in a big way with career highs in goals (35), assists (57) and points (92) in 2017–18. It was an improvement of 40 points over the year prior, 31 points more than his closest teammate, and enough to tie him for seventh in league scoring. The career year earned Kopitar his second Selke Trophy, and he was one of three finalists for the Hart Trophy as NHL MVP.

In the 2018–19 season Kopitar played over 80 games for the eighth time to reach 1,000 games played for his career, and with 60 points he topped the Kings' scoring list once again. By the end of 2018–19, he had accumulated 312 goals and 888 points in his NHL career, while being a plus-70.

Playoff glory may be in the Kings' rearview mirror — they finished last in the Western Conference in 2018–19 — but they have a rare and magical hockey creature to lead them back.

Played in four NHL All-Star Games (2008, 2011, 2015, 2018)

Won the Stanley Cup twice (2012, 2014)

Won the Lady Byng Trophy in 2016

Won the Frank J. Selke Trophy twice (2016, 2018)

Named Hart Trophy finalist in 2018

CONNOR McDAVID

In 2015 Edmonton officially stopped calling itself the City of Champions. Posted on signs entering the city, the slogan celebrated the community's response to a 1987 tornado and the hockey team that was in the midst of winning five Stanley Cups. City councillors might have been premature in voting to remove the signs, however. In 2015 the Oilers drafted the most hyped player since Sidney Crosby.

Growing up in Newmarket, Ontario, Connor McDavid always played with older kids, and his York Simcoe Express team won provincial championships in novice, minor atom, atom, minor peewee and peewee. He left to attend what's now known as Blyth Academy Downsview Park, School for Elite Athletes, in Toronto. There he proved he didn't have just hockey intellect; he also moved up a year academically.

At 15 McDavid became the third player ever to be granted exceptional player status to join the Ontario Hockey League a year early. The Erie Otters took him first overall, and McDavid won back-to-back OHL and Canadian Hockey League Scholastic Player of the Year awards in 2014 and 2015.

In 2014–15 McDavid won both the OHL and CHL Player of the Year honors, despite missing six weeks with a broken hand. The injury caused a national crisis when it appeared he might not play in the World Juniors, but his cast came off days before it started and he had a tournament-leading eight assists in seven games as Canada won the gold.

McDavid finished the OHL season with 44 goals, 120 points and a plus-60 rating in only 47 games, and he added 49 points in 20 playoff games as the Otters lost to the Oshawa Generals in the final.

Crosby was McDavid's idol, and once McDavid hit the NHL he proved he was Crosby's heir apparent. Crosby admits the 6-foot-1, 193-pound center is "far and away the fastest guy I've seen," which was proven when McDavid broke the 21-year-old record for fastest skater at the 2017 All-Star Skills Competition.

His breathtaking speed is one of the reasons McDavid missed almost half of his rookie season in

- Won gold at the 2015 World Junior Championship
- Won gold at the 2016 World Championship
- Won the Hart Trophy in 2017
- Won the Art Ross Trophy and Ted Lindsay Award in 2017 and 2018
- Played in three NHL All-Star Games (2017, 2018, 2019)

2015–16. He was about to blow by two Philadelphia Flyers defenders in a November game when he flew full speed into the end boards, broke his collarbone and missed 37 games. He still finished third in Calder Trophy voting after getting 48 points in 45 games.

Prior to the 2016–17 season, the Oilers named McDavid captain at 19 years, 266 days old, making him the youngest captain in NHL history. As the Second Coming of Wayne Gretzky, McDavid led the league with 70 assists and won the Art Ross Trophy with an even 100 points in his second season. At just 20 McDavid received the Hart Trophy as MVP.

And for the first time in a decade, the Oilers were back in the playoffs. It was a short-lived resurgence, however. Despite McDavid winning the Art Ross again in 2017–18, with 41 goals and 108 points, the Oilers missed the playoffs. He was later named the best player in the game by his peers, winning his second straight Ted Lindsay Award.

But it was small consolation for the ultra-competitive McDavid, who has become a generational talent stuck in a shambolic franchise. When the Oilers were eliminated from playoff contention in 2019, the third time in his four NHL seasons, McDavid spoke out, calling his frustration level "really high. It's really, really high." It was a rare but important call out to the front office and ownership, showing that his endless talent doesn't come with unlimited patience.

"It's been an insane season," added McDavid, who signed an eight-year, $100 million contract starting in 2018–19. "Coaching change. GM change. Good times and bad times. It's been a roller coaster. It's been emotionally challenging."

And it even got worse. During the final game of the season, in which he finished second in points with a career-high 116, McDavid's speed hurt him again. Clocked at 26 miles per hour and bearing down on the Calgary Flames' net, McDavid was knocked down by Mark Giordano and his left leg crashed hard into the post. He didn't get up. When the trainers arrived McDavid could be seen saying, "It's broken."

Luckily for the Oilers it was a knee injury that the team said wouldn't require surgery, but he might as well have been referring to the state of the franchise.

Those "City of Champions" signs can probably stay in storage a little while longer.

BRENT BURNS

The list of things that Brent Burns is at or near the top of in the NHL includes thickest beard, most teeth missing, most tattoo coverage, largest menagerie and most points scored.

Looking through his annual NHL photos is like going through a flipbook of a Teen Wolf transformation. And yes, his body is a colorful mosaic of art and he once had 300 or so snakes, including some rare varieties he crossbred. But focusing on his eccentricities does a disservice to the work ethic that propelled Burns to the NHL.

"He wasn't a very elegant skater. He was bent over like a hunchback toward the ice," recalled Jari Byrski, a skills coach who first met Burns when he was 8 years old. "The thing with Brent is he was always about energy. I'm not talking about a crazy kid not paying attention. Absolutely not. When he set out to do something, he did it the right way and didn't go halfway. He was all in."

Burns was a 5-foot-11 winger when the Brampton Battalion chose him in the third round of the 2001 Ontario Hockey League draft. When training camp started, he was 6-foot-2. "I still think of myself as a small player," said Burns, who is now 6-foot-5 and 230 pounds. "I think it helped my skating and my puckhandling."

After Burns played just one season at forward with the Battalion in 2002–03, the Minnesota Wild took him with the 20th overall selection in the 2003 NHL Entry Draft. He made quite a first impression, walking on stage in a white suit. "He looked like the guys from Dumb and Dumber," said Battalion coach Stan Butler.

Burns also impressed in his first NHL training camp. He made the Wild, and his legend began to grow in Minnesota. Off the ice he became known for his esoteric pursuits like Eastern culture and martial arts, as well as for growing his hair and collecting reptiles; on the ice he'd been converted into a defenseman and set a team record for blue-liners in 2010–11 with 46 points.

Then, in a draft day deal in 2011, the Wild sent Burns to San Jose. The Sharks moved him back to forward during the 2012–13 season but soon realized they were better served with him on the ice more frequently.

In 2015–16 Burns set a new career high with 75 points and became just the fourth defenseman in the past 20 years to reach the 25-goal mark, scoring 27, many on his trademark snapshot that he favors over the booming slap shot. He also joined Bobby Orr and Ray Bourque as the only defensemen with at least 350 shots in a season — his 353 were second to Alex Ovechkin's 398.

In the 2016 playoffs Burns had 24 points in 24 games as the Sharks reached their first Stanley Cup Final, ultimately losing to the Pittsburgh Penguins.

Burns spent that off-season roaming the United States on his custom-made all-black road bicycle, while his family followed in their matte black Mercedes van. He'd work out in Walmart parking lots and at the homes of people they met along the way. Finding his own Route 88 was a way to free his mind and spirit, while pushing his body outside the confines of a gym. It paid off for Burns in 2016–17. The Barrie, Ontario, native led all defensemen with 29 goals, 12 more than the next blue-liner, and 76 points, which earned him the Norris Trophy.

In 2018–19 Burns set new career highs in assists (67), good for fifth in the NHL, and points (83), both of which were first among defensemen. He led the Sharks in scoring for the second year in a row and his was the highest point total by a defenseman since Brian Leetch in 1995–96. He also scored his 14th career overtime goal, breaking Scott Niedermayer's

NHL record for defensemen, and topped the year off with another Norris Trophy nomination.

The last time the 34-year-old Burns missed a game was 2013. Entering the 2019–20 season he was at 471 consecutive and counting, and he's played in over 1,000 games during his career.

The self-described "goofy donkey" has proven he's more than a toothless yeti whose beard has inspired multiple Twitter accounts and a Chia Pet giveaway. Since his first full NHL season he leads all defensemen with 643 points, 60 more than second-place Duncan Keith.

He's quite simply one of the NHL's best players.

Played in six NHL All-Star Games (2011, 2015, 2016, 2017, 2018, 2019)
Won gold at the 2015 World Championship and named best defenseman
Named NHL Foundation Player of the Year in 2015
Won the 2016 World Cup of Hockey
Won the Norris Trophy in 2017

MARK GIORDANO

Named to the CHL All-Rookie Team in 2003

Named captain of the Calgary Flames in 2013

Played in two NHL All-Star Games (2015, 2016)

Received the NHL Foundation Player Award in 2016

Won the Norris Trophy in 2019

As the participants in the Battle of Alberta diverge — the Calgary Flames finished the 2018–19 season first in the Western Conference while the Edmonton Oilers missed the playoffs for the 12th time in 13 seasons — the two provincial captains are also diametrically opposed.

While the Oilers are captained by decorated 22-year-old Connor McDavid, the Flames' Mark Giordano is a no-nonsense defenseman, a late bloomer in his mid-30s. Their paths to the NHL couldn't have been more different. McDavid is a wunderkind who was an instant superstar. Giordano, not so much.

A Toronto, Ontario, native, Giordano went undrafted in 2001, which wasn't surprising since he hadn't played any major junior hockey. He ended up walking on to the Owen Sound Attack of the Ontario Hockey League as a 19-year-old after a tryout.

Two Calgary scouts saw potential in Giordano and recommended him to then-general manager Darryl Sutter. "My first contract was a three-way contract — NHL, AHL and ECHL," explained Giordano. "Darryl Sutter was honest. He said, 'This is pretty much a take-it-or-leave-it-offer.' But he also said, 'If you play well enough, I don't care where you were drafted, or if you were drafted, you'll get a chance.'"

Giordano took the offer and debuted in 2005–06. Early the next season he played his first NHL game in Toronto. It was a memorable night for Maple Leafs fans. Mats Sundin scored his 500th career goal, to complete his hat trick, and was chosen first star.

Lost among the celebrations were Giordano's first and second career NHL goals. "It was a great game," recalled Giordano. "I was second star. Sundin got first star and I got second, and I remember coming out and I got booed."

Giordano split the next two seasons between the Flames and their American Hockey League affiliate. In 2007–08, after his Flames contract expired, he accepted a one-year deal with the Moscow Dynamo of the Kontinental Hockey League. "The risky

things, I always believed they would work out, if you worked hard and played well enough," said Giordano.

It was worth the gamble. After that season Calgary offered him a three-year deal with no minor-league provisions, and Giordano has been a regular on the blue line since. In 2013 the undrafted defenseman succeeded future Hall of Famer Jarome Iginla as captain.

In 2014–15, the defense-first Giordano also added some offense. He was leading all defensemen in scoring and was a Norris Trophy favorite when a biceps tear in a February game ended his season. The following year he had 21 goals and 35 assists in 82 games, tying for second among NHL defensemen in goals and sixth in points.

Then in 2018–19, after seasons of 39 and 38 points, the 35-year-old Giordano had 74 points, 18 more than his previous career high. He led the NHL with a plus-39, was second among defensemen in scoring and was just the fourth defenseman in NHL history with 70 or more points at the age of 35.

"At the same time that I have been getting older, I have become more focused," explained Giordano. "I put in a lot of time working out in the off-season. I haven't felt any effects related to age at all."

In the final regular-season game, Giordano took out McDavid as he charged to the net. McDavid crashed into the post and injured his knee, and after the game Giordano said he felt "terrible."

They're both fiery competitors who never take a night off, and with mutual respect McDavid said, "You can't fault Giordano for trying to make a play on the puck."

Then-Flames goalie Mike Smith said, "Mark wears the captain's C for a reason. He is just a warrior. He competes every day like it is his last day in the league. He is a consummate professional."

Giordano was awarded for his tenacity and belated breakthrough offensive season with the 2019 Norris Trophy. Now that he's a major trophy winner maybe the Alberta captains aren't so different after all.

MARC-ANDRÉ FLEURY

PACIFIC DIVISION

Golden Knights | Goalie | 29

The first pick in the 2003 NHL Entry Draft, after the Pittsburgh Penguins traded up from third, Marc-André Fleury was tending goal for Canada at the 2004 World Juniors and showing why he'd been top choice.

A year after being named top goalie at the 2003 World Juniors in Halifax, the native of Sorel, Quebec, and star of the Quebec Major Junior Hockey League's Cape Breton Screaming Eagles was on his way to a repeat. But up 3–1 in the third period of the 2004 gold medal game against the Americans, he let in three goals, including the game-winner — a failed clearing attempt he put in off his own teammate. Team USA's Al Montoya won gold and the goaltending award, but while he became a journeyman, playing for six teams

over nine NHL seasons, Fleury became a legend.

At his first NHL training camp Fleury faced Mario Lemieux, one of the greatest players to ever pull on a jersey. He was so star-struck he kept the puck from his first shot. In his first NHL game, against the Los Angeles Kings at the Igloo in Pittsburgh, he allowed a goal on the first shot but then stopped 46 of the next 47. That resiliency would be a hallmark of his career.

There were some lean early years in Pittsburgh, but the Penguins drafted Evgeni Malkin and Sidney Crosby in consecutive years and started building a dynasty. In 2008 they lost to a Detroit Red Wings team stocked with legends in the Stanley Cup Final, but in a rematch one year later Fleury stopped a wide-open Nicklas Lidstrom — Hall of Famer and seven-time Norris Trophy winner — with seconds left in Game 7 to seal the 2009 championship.

When Pittsburgh won the Stanley Cup again in 2016 Matt Murray was the number one goalie. The following year they split time on the 2017 championship run, but the Penguins decided to stick with a newer model in Murray, who is 10 years younger, and left Fleury unprotected in the expansion draft.

After 13 seasons, 375 wins in the regular season and another 62 in the playoffs, Fleury was available. The grateful Vegas Golden Knights snapped him up, giving them instant legitimacy and leadership.

Motivated and refreshed by the change in 2017–18, Fleury was third in the NHL in goals-against average (2.24) and tied for sixth in save percentage (.927) with Vezina Trophy winner Pekka Rinne.

In the postseason all Fleury did was lead the first-year team to the Stanley Cup Final with a jaw-dropping .947 save percentage, 1.68 goals-against average and four shutouts through the first three rounds. It was his fifth trip to the final and one of the most unlikely playoff runs in NHL history.

The Cinderella season ended when the Washington Capitals eliminated the Golden Knights in five games, but Fleury was back in top form in 2018–19. He was second in the NHL in shutouts with eight and his 35 wins tied him with Carey Price for fifth. He also passed Jacques Plante for eighth on the all-time wins list and has a shot at joining the top 3, all of whom hail from Quebec. Martin Brodeur and Patrick Roy – numbers one and two, respectively, ahead of Roberto Luongo — are the reasons he became a goalie in the first place.

Even with all that success, Fleury hasn't changed. "He still has that same smile and that same sweet personality when he lived with us," said Angela Hawkins, who billeted Fleury in Cape Breton, during Vegas' Stanley Cup quest. "As you can see in the games, he still likes to have a lot of fun just like when he was 15 years old . . . He's still the same guy."

The goofy grin and good nature have endeared Fleury to hockey fans of all stripes. They also belie the fact that one of the two things he wants to do before he retires is get in a scrap.

"We don't want him fighting, obviously," said Vegas coach Gerard Gallant. "He's one of the top goalies if not the top goalie in the league. His job is to stop the puck and that's what he does."

The other is to score, as long as it's not an own-goal. Fleury has hit a post and just missed a couple times, and with three more years left on his contract, he has some time.

For now, these remain about the only goals the future Hall of Famer hasn't achieved.

Won silver at the 2003 and 2004 World Junior Championship

Won three Stanley Cups (2009, 2016, 2017)

Won gold at the 2010 Winter Olympics

Played in four NHL All-Star Games (2011, 2015, 2018, 2019)

Was eighth all-time in wins at the end of 2018–19

LEON DRAISAITL

- Named WHL playoff MVP in 2015
- Named MVP at the 2015 Memorial Cup
- Runner-up with Team Europe at the 2016 World Cup of Hockey
- Scored 50 goals in 2018–19
- Played in the 2019 NHL All-Star Game

He was called the German Gretzky before he'd ever suited up for Edmonton, but when Leon Draisaitl did pull on the Oilers jersey he made like Mark Messier.

Edmonton drafted Draisaitl third overall from the Western Hockey League's Prince Albert Raiders in 2014. In his first 37 NHL games, in 2014–15, Draisaitl had just two goals and seven assists, so the Oilers sent him down to the Kelowna Rockets, who had traded for his WHL rights. Back in junior he was named playoff MVP after his 28 points in 19 post-season games sent Kelowna to the Memorial Cup.

The Rockets lost in overtime in the championship game to the Oshawa Generals, but Draisaitl led the Memorial Cup in scoring with four goals and seven points in five games and won the Stafford Smythe Memorial Trophy as tournament MVP.

The following season Draisaitl played just six games with the Bakersfield Condors in the American Hockey League before Edmonton called him up. He scored seven goals and 10 assists in his first 10 games, which made him the first Oiler to start a season with 17 points in 10 games since Messier in 1989–90.

Draisaitl worked on his strength and conditioning in the off-season, and playing with renewed confidence in 2015–16 he finished with 19 goals and 51 points in 72 games. The Oilers missed the playoffs for the 10th straight season, but they had the new Messier to their young Gretzky.

Oilers captain Connor McDavid is the man in Edmonton, Draisaitl the wingman, in a literal sense. Draisaitl plays on McDavid's right side when he's not centering the second line.

The 2016–17 season was a rebirth for the franchise. Playing in a new arena, the Oilers tied for seventh overall in the NHL, and Draisaitl finished eighth in the league with 77 points, on 29 goals and 48 assists.

One person who was not a fan of Draisaitl's breakthrough was the Buffalo Sabres' Jack Eichel. With a goal and an assist in the regular-season finale, Draisaitl averaged 0.939 points per game, which was

10th in the NHL. If Eichel had finished in the top 10 he would have collected a $2 million bonus, but he finished 11th with 0.934 points per game, missing out by 5/1,000ths of a decimal point.

Draisaitl would have his own heart broken a few weeks later. After dispatching the defending Western Conference champion San Jose Sharks in six games in the first round, the Oilers pushed the Anaheim Ducks to Game 7 in the Western Conference semifinals.

In Game 5 the Oilers were up 3–0 but allowed three goals in the final 3:16 of the third period before losing in double overtime. Following that devastating loss, Edmonton came out on fire in Game 6, led by Draisaitl. He had the first playoff hat trick by an Oiler since 2000 and two assists in the 7–1 win, putting him second in playoff scoring with 16 points, one behind the Pittsburgh Penguins' Evgeni Malkin.

Those would be the glory days for these Oilers, who missed the playoffs in the two years following despite the high-scoring exploits of their two leaders.

Draisaitl had 25 goals in 2017–18 and then doubled that in 2018–19, reaching the 50-goal plateau after a stretch of 17 goals in 18 games in the second half of the season and three goals in the final two games. He finished just one behind the Washington Capitals' Alex Ovechkin for the Maurice Richard Trophy.

A versatile player who tends to pass when he's at center and shoot when he's on McDavid's wing, Draisaitl became the first player since Malkin in 2011–12 to have at least 50 goals and 100 points in a season.

Draisaitl was also the first person not named Ovechkin to score 50 since Steven Stamkos did it in 2011–12. It was the first time an Oiler had 50 since Gretzky and Jari Kurri, another European-born superstar, each hit the 50-goal mark in 1986–87.

Those two had a host of other future Hall of Famers behind them, including Messier and Glenn Anderson, the other two players in franchise history who had 50 goals in a season, on their way to their third Stanley Cup in four years.

Today's Oilers fans will have to comfort themselves with memories past and bearing witness to the German Gretzky, who's still just 24 and has now etched his own name in the record book.

JOE PAVELSKI

PACIFIC DIVISION

Sharks | Center | 8

SIGNED

Dallas Stars
on July 1, 2019

- Won silver at the 2010 Olympics
- Led the NHL with 11 game-winning goals in 2015–16
- Played in three NHL All-Star Games (2016, 2017, 2019)
- Captained Team USA at the 2016 World Cup of Hockey

Joe Pavelski was an afterthought in the 2003 NHL Entry Draft. The San Jose Sharks' first pick in the seventh round was Jonathan Tremblay, a winger with one point and 232 penalty minutes in the Quebec Major Junior Hockey League.

Pavelski was taken four spots after him. Playing in Iowa for the Waterloo Black Hawks of the United States Hockey League, he was undersized at 5-foot-11 and not the most fleet of foot. "He can't skate, he's not big enough. He can't skate, he's not big enough," recalled Black Hawks coach P.K. O'Handley of the repetitive knock on Pavelski.

But he was a winner. From Plover, Wisconsin, Pavelski led Stevens Point Area High School to a state championship in 2002 and helped the Black Hawks win the USHL's Clark Cup in 2004.

Pavelski joined the University of Wisconsin for the 2004–05 season and in his sophomore year he led the team in assists (33) and points (56) as the Badgers won the 2006 Frozen Four championship. "It's his hands and the six inches between his ears that really elevate his play," according to Wisconsin's coach at the time, Mike Eaves.

Pavelski turned pro in 2006 and had 26 points in just 16 games with the Worcester Sharks in the American Hockey League. He was called up to San Jose, never to return, and scored in his NHL debut.

In 2010 Pavelski proved that he belonged among the best in the world at the Vancouver Olympics. Down a goal to the Canadians in the gold medal game, he won the faceoff for the U.S. and held the offensive zone for Zach Parise's late equalizer. The Americans lost in overtime, but Pavelski went home with a silver medal and a new level of self-confidence.

Pavelski was named Sharks captain in 2015 and in his first year as official leader, he finished fifth in the NHL with 38 goals and appeared in his first All-Star Game. Then, after years of San Jose underachieving in the playoffs, he had nine points in six games in the Western Conference Final to take the Sharks to the 2016 Stanley Cup Final, the franchise's first, where

they lost in six games to the Pittsburgh Penguins.

"All he cares about is winning," said coach Peter DeBoer. "There's not a selfish bone in his body as far as his own personal numbers or agenda. It's all about winning."

In 2018–19 Pavelski led the Sharks with 38 goals, becoming the second player drafted in the seventh round with at least five seasons of 30-plus goals and the second with 10 or more seasons of 20-plus goals. Since 2013–14 he's sixth in the NHL with 205 goals, only three behind second-place Sidney Crosby. But it's in the playoffs when Pavelski really shows his worth, even when he's not on the ice.

In the first round of the 2019 playoffs the Sharks were down 3–0 to the Vegas Golden Knights in the third period of Game 7. With 10:47 left Pavelski was cross-checked off the faceoff by Vegas' Cody Eakin and tumbled backward, cutting his head open after hitting the ice and suffering a concussion. Eakin was called for a hotly debated five-minute major, and vet-

eran Joe Thornton demanded his teammates avenge the loss of their beloved captain.

What followed was the most improbable and thrilling comeback in playoff history; the Sharks scored four times on the power play and eventually won the game 5–4 in overtime.

After missing the first six games of the second round because of the injury, Pavelski returned with a goal and an assist in a 3–2 Game 7 victory over the Colorado Avalanche.

Following a third-round loss to the St. Louis Blues, it was the end of the road for Pavelski in San Jose; after 355 goals and 406 assists in 963 games as a Shark — each top four in franchise history — the free agent signed with the Dallas Stars.

The Stars were seeking leadership and goals to put them over the top, and coach Jim Montgomery knows Pavelski has both in spades: "Because of his details, his habits, he's a perfectionist. It's not by fluke that he scores 38 goals at the age of 34."

ELIAS PETTERSSON

The Swedish pipeline has been good to the Vancouver Canucks, from twins Henrik and Daniel Sedin, the all-time leaders in games played for the franchise, to long-time captain Markus Naslund. They're the top 3 scorers in team history, and based on Elias Pettersson's first season it seems Sweden has bequeathed another candidate to join them.

Pettersson was born in Sundsvall and raised in Ange, where the prodigy had the time and tools to sharpen his craft. His father, Torbjorn, was the Zamboni driver at the local rink, and it gave young Elias plenty of time to skate on his own. But the town didn't have a junior hockey team, so he left home at 15 and played four seasons in the Timra IK system.

Taken fifth overall by Vancouver in 2017, it was over the draft weekend that the Canucks knew they hadn't chosen your average hockey player. As the rounds passed, Pettersson joined the team's brain trust at their draft table to ask about their subsequent selections.

It's almost unheard of, but Pettersson has a curious mind and a commitment to improving his new team.

Before joining Vancouver, however, he played another year in the Swedish Hockey League with Vaxjo HC. As a 19-year-old he dominated against men, winning the regular-season scoring title, with 56 points in 44 games, and league MVP. It set a new SHL scoring record for a player under 20, even after missing games to help Sweden win silver at the World Juniors. He eclipsed Kent Nilsson, who'd held the record since 1976, and passed the Sedins, Naslund and Peter Forsberg along the way.

Vaxjo won the SHL championship, and Pettersson led the playoffs in scoring with 19 points in 13 games, setting another record for a junior-aged SHL player, ahead of the Sedins, Anze Kopitar and previous holder Axel Holmstrom.

After winning the Stefan Liv Memorial Trophy as playoff MVP Pettersson took the European golden helmet for top scorer one step further and painted his whole body gold. It was a fitting prelude; Pettersson then joined Sweden at the World Championship and added a gold medal to his already impressive résumé.

There was little doubt Pettersson would be in the Canucks lineup on opening night of the 2018–19 season, and he didn't disappoint. Playing at center when logic and pundits suggested starting his career on the wing, he quickly earned his place in the lineup and the hearts of fans with a highlight reel goal that ignited the crowd and led to a win over the Calgary Flames. Suddenly a season that began with low expectations after the Canucks finished second last in the Western Conference in 2017–18 had hope.

"You look at him and he's 170-something pounds and it doesn't matter if it's a slap shot or a wrist shot, he just crushes it," said teammate Troy Stecher. "His first goal against Calgary, he doesn't lose stride and he cocks it way back. It looked like he was going to pass it, and the next thing I know, he slingshots it into the net.

"I've never seen anything like that."

Pettersson's shot was once seen as a potential weakness, but he broke it down and built it up to turn it into a strength. Light and lanky with long arms and quick hands, he can dangle and change angles to confuse defenders and goalies. It gives him an unpredictable shot and the ability to pull off audacious dekes in a shootout. He's a hockey savant who makes plays others don't even think about or have the confidence to try.

According to teammate Jake Virtanen, the whole bench is constantly dumbstruck by something Pettersson does on the ice. "It happens once a game, at least."

Pettersson is also a conscientious backchecker, a rarity for such an offensive talent, especially a young one.

The Calder Trophy for rookie of the year was Pettersson's to lose after he scored 10 goals in his first 10 games, a run that was interrupted by the physical reality of the NHL. He suffered a concussion on a borderline hit by the Florida Panthers' Mike Matheson that finished with a body slam. He sat for six games and also missed time in January with a sprained right knee.

Pettersson finished the season tops among all freshmen with 28 goals and 66 points in 71 games, 21 more points than rookie runner-up Brady Tkachuk of the Ottawa Senators. It broke the franchise record for rookie scoring held by legends Pavel Bure and Ivan Hlinka and earned him the Calder Trophy.

Teammates took to calling Pettersson "Alien" early, after seeing his otherworldly talents up close. But E.P. didn't come from above, just northern Sweden.

Won silver at the 2018 World Junior Championship

Won gold at the 2018 World Championship

Played in the 2019 NHL All-Star Game

Won the Calder Trophy in 2019

DREW DOUGHTY

Exhibit A in the argument for east coast bias is the Kings' Drew Doughty. If hockey writers in the east couldn't stay up late enough to get a true measure of the talent in the west, they were missing out on one of the league's best players in Los Angeles.

Doughty's 2016 Norris Trophy as the NHL's best defenseman was years overdue, but the individual bauble was just icing on the cake. He'd already won every important championship (some twice) by the time it finally came his way.

Growing up in London, Ontario, Doughty dreamed of hoisting the World or FA Cups just as much as Lord Stanley's. His mother, Connie, is Portuguese and his father, Paul, is English, so soccer was a household passion.

Though Doughty was a standout soccer goalie, he made the difficult decision to focus on hockey at the age of 15. "I was just as good at soccer as I was at hockey," recalled Doughty. "But living in Canada, it's going to be tough to make it [in soccer] anywhere. So I kind of gave it up. I miss playing it all the time."

Paul believes the two sports worked together in his son's favor: "I actually think playing soccer helped him with hockey. He could sit back in net and watch the whole play develop in front of him."

At 17 Doughty led the Ontario Hockey League's Guelph Storm in scoring in 2006–07, with 74 points in 67 games. A year later he won the Max Kaminsky Trophy as the OHL's most outstanding defenseman and was named the top blue-liner at the 2008 World Junior Championship after Canada won gold.

Later that year LA picked Doughty second overall in the entry draft, and after his fitness was questioned he dropped 20 pounds during the summer. He made the team out of training camp and played his first game for the Kings at 18, the second-youngest defenseman in franchise history. Conditioning wasn't an issue; Doughty averaged almost 24 minutes a game his rookie year. "It's not junior anymore," said Sean O'Donnell, Doughty's first NHL defense partner and mentor. "Playing against men, you'll get fatigued and that's when you get hurt.

"[Doughty] understood the game, he understood the nuances. It usually takes defensemen years to do that and some never get it. To see him do that as a 19-year-old, you knew he was special."

In 2010 Doughty was a finalist for the Norris at 20 years old, the second youngest to be nominated for the award, after Bobby Orr. He had helped the Kings reach the playoffs for the first time in eight years. He was also the youngest member of Canada's gold medal Olympic team. Over the course of the tournament he moved up the depth chart to form the team's top defense tandem with Duncan Keith.

Two years later, as the Kings steamrolled their way to the franchise's first championship, Doughty's 16 points in 20 playoff games led all blue-liners, and his 26:08 of average ice time was almost a minute more than anyone else in the Stanley Cup Final.

In 2014, after adding a second gold medal to his trophy case at the Sochi Olympics, Doughty topped all defensemen again with 18 points in the playoffs as the Kings won their second Stanley Cup.

The 2016–17 season started with more international titles, this time at the World Cup of Hockey, but ended with the Kings on the outside of the playoffs looking in. The following season they were swept in the first round by the expansion Vegas Golden Knights, but Doughty still finished second in Norris Trophy voting.

That summer, Doughty, who grew up a Kings fan in southern Ontario, toyed with fans of the Toronto Maple Leafs about the idea of a homecoming as free agency approached in 2019. In the end he chose the Kings, signing an eight-year, $88 million contract to stay in LA.

Doughty didn't figure in the Norris conversation in 2019, but he believed his defensive game improved, and he was still voted the second-best defenseman in the league by his peers in the NHLPA's annual player poll. He also came second in the best trash talker and funniest player categories.

Doughty shows up to work every night — he hasn't missed a game since 2014–15 — even in a difficult season. The Kings missed the 2019 playoffs by a considerable margin while the Leafs became an Eastern Conference contender, one elite defenseman short of being a Cup favorite. Despite that, he said he never really considered leaving the only professional home he's ever known.

The refreshingly frank star even admitted he didn't want the Kings to get complacent and lowball him in contract talks. And it's a pretty nice life on the west coast. The hockey spotlight is a little less bright, and the sun always shines on his $6 million Hermosa Beach home.

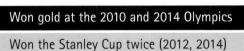

Won gold at the 2010 and 2014 Olympics

Won the Stanley Cup twice (2012, 2014)

Played in five NHL All-Star Games (2015, 2016, 2017, 2018, 2019)

Won the Norris Trophy in 2016

Won the 2016 World Cup of Hockey

ERIK KARLSSON

When Erik Karlsson admitted to reporters during the 2017 playoffs that he had two hairline fractures in his left heel, he broke serious and longstanding protocol. The don't ask, don't tell policy for injuries in the postseason prevents your opponent from targeting your weakness, but as Karlsson said, "I'm not much for secrets."

In the Senators' Cinderella playoff run, opponents weren't going to slow Karlsson down anyway — he was their Achilles' heel.

Karlsson had been injured blocking a shot, an occupational hazard for a player with 201 blocks, the second most in 2016–17. His tendency to block might also be a result of his original desire to be a goalie, a notion his father crushed when he was 6.

Jonas Karlsson was a lumberjack in Landsbro in the south Swedish highlands and a defenseman in Sweden's top league, so when he dressed his son up in

full goalie gear and wound up for a slap shot it scared young Erik right out of the net.

Playing defense, Karlsson was signed by Sodertalje SK when he was 16, but he was homesick and lasted only 10 games (getting 10 points) before joining Frolunda and winning Sweden's junior title in 2008.

Karlsson also played for Team Sweden and coach Anders Forsberg at the Under-18 World Championship in 2008. The Senators hired Forsberg as a scout soon after, and together with head scout Pierre Dorion they encouraged then-general manager Bryan Murray to move up in the 2008 NHL Entry Draft to get him. At 5-foot-10, 157 pounds and looking like "a 12-year-old boy," according to Dorion, it took some convincing.

When Karlsson joined the Senators in 2009 his fluid skating and offensive acumen were obvious, but his defense and size were a work in progress. In 2011 then-coach Paul MacLean said Karlsson was capable of 30 minutes a night, as long as he's not "playing 14 minutes for us and 16 minutes for them."

It was a commentary on Karlsson's risk-taking playing style, which has produced some impressive numbers. In 2011–12, at 22 years old, he won his first Norris Trophy after his 78 points led all defensemen by a whopping 25. He was the second Swede to be named best defenseman, after Nicklas Lidstrom, one of his idols, and only the third player under 23, after Bobby Orr and Denis Potvin.

Karlsson was first among defensemen in points again in 2013–14 (74) and 2014–15 (66), when he won his second Norris Trophy. A third seemed likely in 2015–16 when he was first in the entire NHL in assists (66) and fourth in points (82) — the first time a defenseman had finished top 5 in scoring since 1985–86. But he ended up losing to Drew Doughty, who had 31 fewer points.

Already one of the game's best defensemen, Karlsson showed he was one of the best leaders in the 2017 playoffs. He had 16 assists and 18 points in 19 games to take the Senators to the Eastern Conference Final. His two goals were both game-winners, and he had two defining moments.

In Game 2 of the first round against the Boston Bruins, cameras caught Karlsson yelling at teammate Derick Brassard. It was a rare moment of pique for the cool captain but a well-chosen one. Brassard tied the game in the third period, with a jaw-dropping assist from Karlsson, of course, before Ottawa won in overtime. "We looked at each other after the goal and we said, 'Are we good now, we good?'" laughed Brassard after the game.

It might've been the last laugh Karlsson had in Ottawa. The following season the Senators plummeted to second last in the NHL, and Karlsson escaped the tire fire at the Canadian Tire Centre when Dorion, now the general manager, traded him to the San Jose Sharks prior to the 2018–19 season. With a year left on his contract, the team didn't want to risk losing their franchise leader in goals, assists and points by a defenseman for nothing.

A groin injury limited Karlsson to 53 games with the Sharks, but heading into the 2019–20 season he still led all defensemen in assists (434) and points (563) since entering the NHL, 31 points ahead of teammate Brent Burns.

Having two of the best defensemen in the game wasn't quite enough for the Sharks, however, and Karlsson lost in the conference final for the second time in his career.

A much-coveted free agent at season's end, Karlsson decided he liked the sun, sand, sea and Silicon Valley and stayed a Shark. There was also some unfinished business with Stanley.

Played in six NHL All-Star Games (2011, 2012, 2016, 2017, 2018, 2019)
Led all NHL defensemen in scoring four times (2011–12, 2013–14, 2014–15, 2015–16)
Won the Norris Trophy twice (2012, 2015)
Won silver at the 2014 Olympics and voted best defenseman

MARTIN JONES

Just a few years after donning the pads full time Martin Jones played at the prestigious Quebec International Pee-Wee Tournament, where players like Guy Lafleur, Wayne Gretzky and Steven Stamkos made a name for themselves.

Every year thousands of fans and scores of scouts come to watch 11- and 12-year-olds, hoping to catch a glimpse of future NHL stars. In 2003 they saw a cool young Jones lead his North Shore Winter Club Winterhawks to one of the divisional titles.

"When you watched him play, you literally wouldn't know if he had a shutout or had let in four," said Billy Coupland, Jones' coach for five years. "It was like he was back home playing in front of friends and family."

In 2005 the North Vancouver team won the bantam provincial title and Jones allowed just a single goal in six games in the year-end tournament. Over

five seasons together the Winterhawks went 98-2 in the Pacific Coast Amateur Hockey Association and won the league title each year.

Still just 5-foot-8 when he was eligible for the Western Hockey League draft in 2005, Jones wasn't taken until the fourth round by the Calgary Hitmen. He was relegated to the backup role, where he remained in 2008 when he was passed over in the NHL Entry Draft. "He was disappointed," said his father, Harvey. "But he doesn't let things like that knock him. He wouldn't accept failure."

By then Jones had grown to 6-foot-4 and earned a tryout with the Los Angeles Kings, in part because his former backup in North Vancouver was Dylan Crawford, son of Marc Crawford, LA's coach at the time. Jones impressed and was offered an entry-level contract.

Sent back to the WHL Jones inherited the number one job with the Hitmen and ran with it. In 2010 he won the WHL's best goaltender and playoff MVP awards on his way to being named the top goaltender at the Memorial Cup.

Jones finally made his NHL debut on December 3, 2013, a victory over the Anaheim Ducks, and then reeled off seven more wins in a row, which tied the record for most consecutive wins to start a career set by the Philadelphia Flyers' Bob Froese in 1982–83. Over that stretch Jones had a 0.98 goals-against average, a .966 save percentage and three shutouts.

Jones played 19 games backing up Jonathan Quick in 2013–14, with a 1.81 goals-against average, a .934 save percentage and four shutouts. He also played 56 minutes over two games in the playoffs to get his named etched on the Stanley Cup with the 2014 champion Kings.

With Quick ensconced as the Kings' starter, Jones was traded in June 2015 — twice. First he was sent to the Boston Bruins and four days later the Bruins traded him to the San Jose Sharks, who immediately signed him to a three-year, $9 million contract.

The Sharks were vindicated as Jones set a franchise record with a shutout streak of 234 minutes and 33 seconds in October 2015. He finished the season third in the NHL with 37 wins and second with six shutouts.

But it was in the playoffs that he really thrilled. Jones had back-to-back shutouts in the Western Conference Final against the St. Louis Blues to help the Sharks reach their first Stanley Cup Final. He made 44 saves in Game 5, the most in an elimination game in Cup final history, before the Sharks bowed out in six games to the Pittsburgh Penguins.

In the 2018–19 season Jones tied for third in the NHL in victories (36) and became the first goalie in franchise history with four straight 30-plus-win seasons. But questions were raised after some inconsistent starts, to put it generously, that bled into the playoffs.

Yet Jones has made a habit of answering his critics and he did so emphatically. In his last three games against the Vegas Golden Knights in the first round he had a .946 save percentage — including a record-setting 58 saves in Game 6, a 2–1 double-overtime win — as the Sharks rallied from being down three games to one to win the series.

It was part of a 10-game stretch in which he was 7-3 with a 2.13 goals-against average and .928 save percentage, winning four elimination games with a .949 save percentage, including two Game 7s.

"They should have a stat that says 'belief in your goaltender,'" said Sharks coach Peter DeBoer before the playoffs. "If they had that stat, Jonesy would be batting 1.000 with our group. There's not been one mumble or whisper within our group about him or our confidence in him to get the job done."

Named the WHL's best goaltender and playoff MVP in 2010

Named best goaltender at the Memorial Cup in 2010

Won the Stanley Cup in 2014

Won gold at the 2015 World Championship

Played in the 2017 NHL All-Star Game

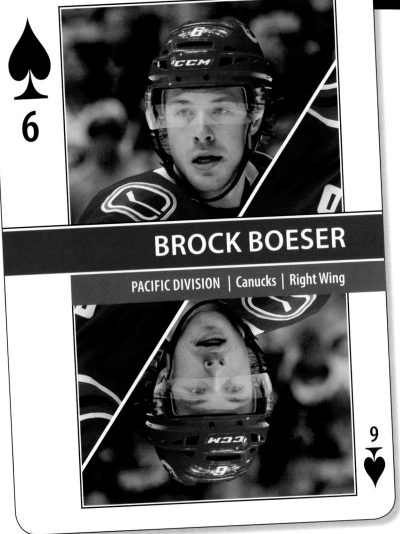

BROCK BOESER

PACIFIC DIVISION | Canucks | Right Wing

lead with 35 goals and third with 68 points.

Through this all, he was also watching his father, Duke, suffer from Parkinson's disease.

"Brock's just one of those kids we've learned that is very sensitive and caring, but he's also very focused and can persevere through anything," said his mother, Laurie. "He's had some stuff to deal with. Very good stuff and some hard stuff for a young guy."

Boeser went on to play for the University of North Dakota, scoring 43 goals and 94 points in 74 games over two seasons and helping the Fighting Hawks win the 2016 NCAA championship.

Selected 23rd overall by the Vancouver Canucks in 2015, Boeser signed his first contract on March 25, 2017, the day after North Dakota was eliminated from the NCAA tournament. He scored the game-winner later that day against the Minnesota Wild in his home state and was named first star, but even better was having his mother and father in the dressing room to read out the starting lineup, featuring their son at right wing.

n August 2014 Brock Boeser was in Slovakia representing the U.S. at the Hlinka Gretzky Cup when he heard that four close friends from Burnsville High School were in a car accident back in Minnesota. Baseball teammate Ty Alyea had been killed.

Boeser's coaches gave him permission to go home, but the captain made the difficult decision to stay and promised Alyea's mother he'd score for Ty on the day of the wake. He did and went on to tie for the tournament lead in goals as Team USA captured bronze.

That fall Boeser faced another deep loss when he learned of his grandfather's death hours before he made his debut for the Waterloo Black Hawks in the United States Hockey League. He scored again that night for his "G-pa" and ended the season tied for the USHL

Boeser's four goals over the last nine games of the season were a sign of things to come. In 2017–18 he scored two goals in his first three games and was named the Rookie of the Month in November after leading all NHL players with 11 goals.

Boeser won again in December when he had eight goals and 13 points in 13 games. He reached the 20-goal mark two days before Christmas and had 25 goals in his first 44 NHL games, 11 games quicker than Hall of Famer and former Canuck Pavel Bure. He also became the first Canucks rookie since Trevor Linden to have a hat trick.

Henrik Sedin, the franchise's all-time leading scorer, who was playing in his final NHL season, called Boeser the best pure finisher he'd seen since arriving in Vancouver in 2000.

Among the league leaders in goals, Boeser was picked for the All-Star Game, and the rookie proved he belonged among the best, winning the accuracy shooting competition and the All-Star Game MVP award.

The dream season was derailed by a hit from the New York Islanders' Cal Clutterbuck that fractured a bone in Boeser's lower back, which cost him the last 16 games and likely the Calder Trophy. Boeser finished with 29 goals and 55 points in 62 games and was second in Calder voting to Clutterbuck's teammate Mathew Barzal.

Boeser's off-season training was hampered by his back injury, and he struggled with his confidence, skating and shot at the start of the 2018–19 season. He had another setback with a groin injury early in the year, but as the season progressed he developed a strong relationship with rookie Elias Pettersson, on and off the ice.

When Boeser and Pettersson played together the Canucks controlled 65.31 percent of the goals, 60.31 percent of the expected goals and 59.81 percent of the scoring chances; when they didn't it was just 40.27 percent of the goals, 44.45 percent of the expected goals and 41.35 percent of the scoring chances.

The numbers back up their synergy, but it was the raw skill and creativity that will stick in Canucks fans' minds and keep them warm after another year outside the playoffs.

The 6-foot-1, 208-pound Boeser has run the emotional gauntlet and knows that with optimal health, both physical and mental, his ceiling is sky high.

"That excites me," said Boeser at the end of the season. "With the year I had, the ups and downs, and to still get near 30 goals, that's exciting for me. I think I can be a 40-goal scorer in this league.

"I just need to take that next step."

Won bronze at the 2016 World Junior Championship	
Won the NCAA championship in 2016	
Named MVP of the 2018 NHL All-Star Game	
Runner-up for the Calder Trophy in 2018	

SEAN MONAHAN

PACIFIC DIVISION | Flames | Center

Sean Monahan has always been remarkably consistent. From an early age he could find the back of the net, and just as early he didn't want anyone to know about it. Even at the age of 3 he didn't want to stand out on the ice and found ways for his dad to keep him on the bench, at one point telling him the ice was "too slippery."

It was hard for young Monahan to keep a low profile though. "At 6 years old he scored an overtime goal for us to upset the Toronto Marlies," recounted childhood friend and teammate Mike Kussman. "In lacrosse he was always the go-to guy for goals. He was [good for] six goals every game."

When he wasn't filling the net in the Brampton (Ontario) Battalion hockey system or for the lacrosse

Excelsiors, Monahan was excelling at high school sports and academics at St. Thomas Aquinas Secondary School. It was a recipe for youthful confidence and bravado, but Monahan wasn't built that way.

"I don't know what it was," said Monahan. "I wouldn't want to go on the ice, or the floor. Or if I scored a bunch of goals I would just put my head down and come off. Even in class, I would know the answer to the teacher's question and be too shy to put my hand up. It was just something with me."

Monahan, who wore number 19 in minor hockey as a tribute to his two favorite players, Steve Yzerman and Joe Thornton, was drafted in the first round of the 2010 Ontario Hockey League draft, 16th overall, by the Ottawa 67's. He scored 84 goals over three seasons in Ottawa and was in the discussion to go top 3 in the 2013 NHL draft with Nathan MacKinnon and Seth Jones. Even that didn't go to his head.

"What he is is normal," said 67's teammate Brett Gustavsen at the time. "Lots of guys have egos. You see lots of superstars get full of themselves. He is not that. Sean is just so composed and so professional."

Monahan ended up going sixth overall, between Elias Lindholm and Darnell Nurse, and without any time in the minors he scored 22 goals in his rookie season, including four times in the first five games. He was the first Flames rookie to score more than 20 goals since Jarome Iginla in 1996–97.

The 6-foot-2, 200-pound center has had a remarkably similar start to his career as future Hall of Famer Iginla, whose number was retired by the Flames in 2019. Iginla had 174 goals in his first six NHL seasons, while Monahan had 172.

The similarities end there, however; the two players, who are opposite shots, differ significantly in emotional play and physicality. One knock against

Monahan is a perceived lack of passion. There's even a parody Twitter account, @boringmonahan, that has almost 60,000 followers, 23,000 more than Monahan himself.

Maybe with more bluster he'd be a bigger star and silence the critics of his cerebral game, but that's not Monahan's style and no one can argue with the results.

In 2018–19 Monahan had a career-high 34 goals and 82 points, 18 more points than his previous best the season prior and tied with Phil Kessel and Jack Eichel for 23rd in the NHL. He now has more goals than anyone from his draft year, including Hart Trophy finalist MacKinnon and Aleksander Barkov, who were drafted first and second, respectively.

Since entering the league Monahan is tied with Kessel and MacKinnon for eighth in game-winning goals with 35, which puts him fourth in Flames history behind legends Iginla, Theo Fleury and Joe Nieuwendyk. And at just 25 he's already first in overtime goals with 10.

"Since I've been here, it seems like he scores a lot in the third and OT," said teammate Matthew Tkachuk. "He's a clutch player and we're really lucky to have him."

Monahan is not without his quirks — he's extremely superstitious about his equipment — and has started to show glimpses of his true personality with the media. He's even getting more comfortable celebrating goals, if only because they're happening so frequently.

But same old Monahan otherwise.

"People ask me that a lot, 'Has he changed? Does he still come around?'" said Kussman. "He's 100 percent humble and genuine. A loyal friend. Absolutely nothing has changed him.

"I would assume it's a pretty rare thing. Because for a lot of people, naturally, things are going to change. With Sean, absolutely nothing."

- Became the youngest Flame and sixth-youngest player in NHL history (22 years and 134 days old) to reach 100 career goals
- Tied an NHL record with a power-play goal in four straight playoff games in 2017
- Owns the Flames' record for career regular-season overtime goals with 10

MARK STONE

PACIFIC DIVISION | Golden Knights | Right Wing

When Mark Stone was a baby his dad, Rob, played on Saturdays at Sargent Park Arena in Winnipeg, Manitoba. Older brother Michael played on foot with some other kids beside the rink and Mark felt left out.

"Mark wanted to play hockey, too," remembers his mother, Jackie. "But he couldn't walk. So I got him one of those walkers with wheels so he could play by moving his legs around. He'd be up and down with the rest of the kids."

It was fertile training ground for both brothers; Michael has played nine NHL seasons as a defenseman and Mark is a star.

Ultracompetitive as a youngster, Mark was studying game tapes when he was 10. When he was 14

the Brandon Wheat Kings picked Mark 92nd overall in the 2007 Western Hockey League bantam draft. But he still had to grow into his lanky frame, as Kelly McCrimmon, the Wheat Kings' owner, general manager and head coach at the time, recalled years later. "He hadn't, as a young player, added up to the sum of his parts," said McCrimmon. "The skating really needed work, physical maturation, getting stronger. Those were the things that had to come together for him."

They did over Stone's four seasons in Brandon. He had 229 points in 137 games over his final two years, including 41 goals and 123 points in 66 games in 2011–12. He also won bronze with Canada's World Junior team that year, scoring seven goals and 10 points in six games.

Drafted in the sixth round, 178th overall, in 2010 by the Ottawa Senators, two years after the Coyotes took his brother 69th overall, Stone spent two seasons shuttling between Ottawa and its AHL affiliate in Binghamton. After proactively working on his skating he established himself as an NHL regular in 2014–15 with 26 goals and 64 points.

Over the following four seasons Stone did it all — he played on special teams, shut down the opponents' stars and gave rookies a place to live. He was also consistent in his scoring and demeanor, even through Ottawa's wild ups and downs.

The Senators reached the Eastern Conference Final in 2017, but less than two years later they had plummeted all the way to the bottom of the standings. He escaped the sinking ship in Ottawa when the impending free agent was dealt to the Golden Knights at the 2019 trade deadline for a package that included Vegas' top prospect Erik Brannstrom. "Stone is the here, the now, the future," said then-Vegas general manager George McPhee. "He is the type of player you always look for and hope to be able to land."

The Golden Knights reached the Stanley Cup Final in 2018 and went all in to take that final step in 2019. Stone held up his end of the bargain; he was leading the NHL in both goals (6) and points (12) when the San Jose Sharks eliminated them in Game 7.

"There are a lot of guys that I respect in this league," said linemate Paul Stastny after Stone scored his first career hat trick in Game 3. "But the ones I respect most are the ones who think the game, and have that vision and anticipation, and think one step ahead. That's what [Stone] has."

Stone's hockey IQ covers the full extent of the ice, and he was a finalist for the 2019 Selke Trophy as the

NHL's best defensive forward, a rarity for a winger. When he was on the ice for the last-place Senators in 2018–19 they were a remarkable plus-85 in shot attempts, and he finished the season with career highs in goals (33) and points (73).

At 6-foot-4 and 219 pounds he also uses his size for good, not evil, averaging under 23 minutes in penalties a season, and he's led the NHL in takeaways in five of his six seasons.

Stone agreed to a new eight-year, $76 million contract when he was traded, and with new Vegas general manager McCrimmon and childhood friend Cody Eakin on the team it's starting to feel like home.

"When you come here for the first time to play, you get that understanding the fans are incredible," said Stone. "They treat players with first class. Everything in here has been so easy for me."

Fans and management have made Stone happy in Vegas, so he's staying in Vegas.

Named WHL and CHL most sportsmanlike player in 2012

Named to the NHL All-Rookie Team in 2015

Won gold at the 2016 World Championship

Voted a finalist for the Frank J. Selke Trophy in 2019

OLIVER EKMAN-LARSSON

PACIFIC DIVISION | Coyotes | Defense

As a kid in tiny Tingsryd, Sweden, Oliver Ekman-Larsson would set his VCR to tape Detroit Red Wings games that were on late at night so he could watch them the next day after school.

It was a stacked Wings roster with several Swedes and future Hall of Famers, including Sweden's statesman and engine from the back, Nicklas Lidstrom. He was Ekman-Larsson's favorite player and the model for his game growing up.

Defense runs in the family — Ekman-Larsson's grandfather played on the blue line for Sweden at the 1972 Olympics — but Oliver took a shot at center when his dad coached him because his father wanted him to see the ice from a different perspective. He moved back to defense when he joined a higher age group, with a better understanding of the passes his forwards wanted.

At 17 Ekman-Larsson joined Leksands in Sweden's second division, scoring 17 points in 39 games in the 2008–09 season, a league record for players 18 and under. The following year his 27 points led all teenagers in the second division.

The Phoenix Coyotes liked what they saw in Lidstrom-lite and drafted him sixth overall in 2009. In 2010 he won bronze medals with Sweden at both the World Juniors and World Championship before playing his first NHL game.

By the time the 2014 Olympics in Sochi, Russia, came around, Lidstrom had retired and Ekman-Larsson was a rising star in both the NHL and his country. He had three points and was a plus-4 in the tournament — good for second best on the team — as Sweden captured the silver medal.

Back in the desert, Ekman-Larsson finished with 23 goals in 2013–14 to tie Phil Housley's franchise mark for goals by a defenseman and set the record for most goals in a season by a Swedish-born defenseman. In the 2014–15 season he led all NHL defensemen in goals, game-winning goals and power-play goals.

Ekman-Larsson's 43 points in 2014–15 led the Coyotes, and he was the team's top scorer again in 2015–16 with 55 points. He also set an NHL record for defensemen with eight game-winning goals. Being an NHL team's leading scorer twice in a row is a rare feat for any defenseman not named Bobby Orr.

In 2016–17 Ekman-Larsson's upward trajectory dipped a little, the result of playing with a broken left thumb for six weeks while trudging toward a fifth straight season out of the playoffs. He didn't sit out a single game while his thumb healed, and he's only missed 13 games in his NHL career.

Ekman-Larsson had the benefit of watching how

former Coyotes captain Shane Doan dealt with adversity in the NHL. "When I got in the league, I looked to Doaner every game we lost and how he acted or how he handled himself. I think that's huge, especially when we have a lot of young players. I feel that's important."

When Doan retired in 2018, the reins were handed to Ekman-Larsson as the new Coyotes' captain. The team also signed him to an eight-year contract averaging $8.25 million a season. It was a bargain for the slick, smooth-skating defender, who had 14 goals and 44 points in 2018–19, while his 162 hits and 52 blocked shots helped the Coyotes to a tie for the league's best penalty-killing percentage and fifth-lowest goals against. He also led the team in ice time at 23:38 per game despite playing through ankle and knee injuries.

While the Coyotes narrowly missed the playoffs, finishing one spot and four points out, Ekman-Larsson was named a finalist for the King Clancy Memorial Trophy, which recognizes the player who best exemplifies leadership qualities on and off the ice.

It didn't surprise teammate Derek Stepan, who also recognized the lineage of the captaincy: "Off the ice, 'O' is one of the greatest humans I've ever met. I think he got a little bit of Shane Doan to rub off on him. He's got a lot of those qualities. The leading part just comes natural with him."

It also benefits his native country, as Ekman-Larsson helped Sweden to world championship titles in 2017 and 2018, scoring a shootout goal in each gold medal game — and inspiring a young generation of defensemen to come home after school and watch his every move on YouTube.

| Won silver at the 2014 Olympics |
| Led the Coyotes in scoring in 2014–15 and 2015–16 |
| Played in two NHL All-Star Games (2015, 2018) |
| Won gold at the World Championship in 2017 and 2018 |

SHEA THEODORE

PACIFIC DIVISION | Golden Knights | Defense

Shea Theodore learned to skate at the Aldergrove Community Arena, the only rink in the British Columbia town of about 15,000 people. And it's where he played all his hockey through midget, even when bigger teams came calling.

"A lot of kids moved and went to play for winter clubs or that, but I just stayed because I liked my friends and I liked playing close to home," said Theodore. "We only had 24 kids try out for the team every year. Everyone pretty much made the team."

Yet they still made the provincial tournament one season, a huge accomplishment for the little town. It was a theme that would continue into Theodore's pro hockey life, albeit in a city as removed from Aldergrove as North America offers.

Theodore finally left his hometown after being drafted by the Western Hockey League's Seattle Thunderbirds in 2010. At the tender age of 15 he led the Thunderbirds defense with 35 points, then upped that total to 50 and 79 points in the next two seasons.

Drafted 26th overall by the Anaheim Ducks in 2013 Theodore seemed poised to make it to the big club in 2014, but he was injured in training camp and sent back to junior. It was a personal blow but a blessing to his country.

Eligible for the 2015 World Juniors, Theodore was on the top defensive pair with Darnell Nurse. The tandem didn't allow a goal the entire tournament and Canada won gold for the first time in six years.

"The real coming out for him was that World Junior tournament," said Seattle general manager Russ Farwell. "He really established himself as a world class player and man it was a shot of confidence. A lot of guys have a little bit of a letdown after World Juniors, but he really went the other way. He came back confident and saw himself as a world class player and was a dominant player on our team from then on."

Theodore spent the following two seasons bouncing between the NHL and AHL, playing 53 games over two seasons with the Ducks before being traded to the Vegas Golden Knights during the 2017 expansion draft.

The motley crew of castoffs in Sin City made an unprecedented and entertaining run all the way to the Stanley Cup Final, with Theodore earning 10 points in the playoffs, including the first postseason goal in franchise history, against the Los Angeles Kings.

The Golden Knights were vanquished in five games by the Washington Capitals, but the team won over a city, and Theodore had an NHL home, signing a seven-year, $36.4 million contract in the off-season.

"Based on the way he played last year and what he

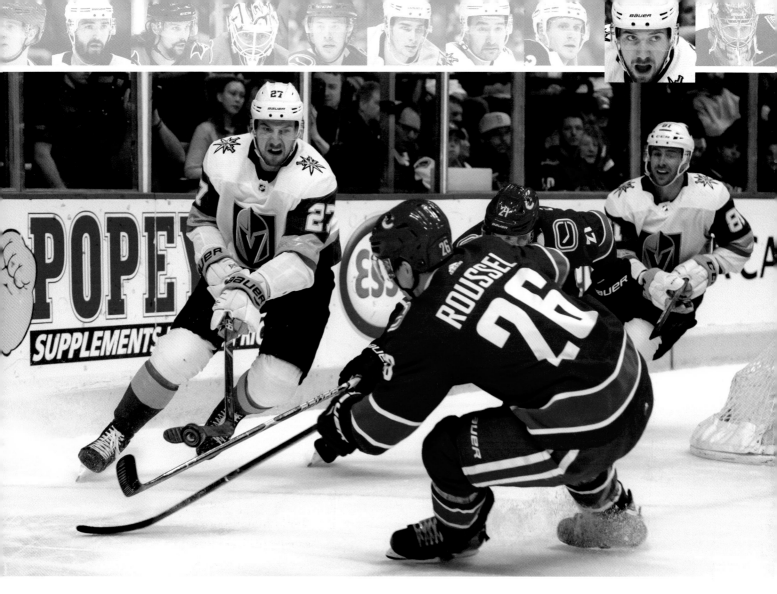

did at his age . . . to really play that well, and to play that well in the playoffs for four rounds, we're pretty confident in what we're going to have now and in the future," said Golden Knights president of hockey operations George McPhee.

A midseason move to the right side in 2018–19, where Theodore played in his last two seasons in Seattle, helped the left-shooting defender become even deadlier. With his blade to the center of the ice, giving him more options with the puck, he had 12 points and was plus-4 in his first 21 games on the right. He finished the season leading the Golden Knights' defense with 12 goals and 37 points.

His already strong possession numbers also went up after the switch. In 2018–19 he had a 57.1 percent Corsi, identical to Norris Trophy winner Mark Giordano. Offensively established, Theodore just has to add the consistency and reliability that are hallmarks of elite NHL defensemen.

"[Theodore] is young, he's got lots of years to improve and get better and bigger and stronger," said fellow Vegas blue-liner and mentor Deryk Engelland. "I don't think we've seen the most of him yet."

After coming oh so close to hockey's holy grail in 2018 and creating a new generation of hockey fans in the desert, Theodore returned home to help open the new Aldergrove Credit Union Community Centre.

Theodore didn't bring the Stanley Cup to town, but he'd already inspired the young players by proving that someone from their small town can make it big.

Won gold at the 2012 Hlinka Gretzky Cup, 2013 Under-18 World Championship and 2015 World Junior Championship

Named WHL West first-team All-Star and Bill Hunter Trophy winner as the league's best defenseman in 2015

Scored the first goal in Golden Knights' playoff history (April 11, 2018, against the Los Angeles Kings)

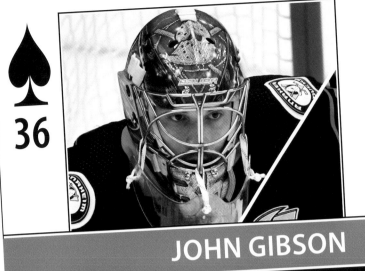

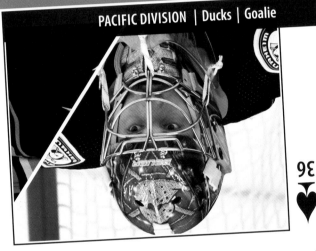

JOHN GIBSON

PACIFIC DIVISION | Ducks | Goalie

The 2018–19 season was one to forget for the Anaheim Ducks, but there was a bright spot between the pipes, where 26-year-old John Gibson plies his trade.

The season started well. The Ducks were jostling for position at the top of the standings and Gibson was an early Vezina Trophy candidate. By January Gibson had become the busiest goalie in the league. He had faced the most shots and made the most saves of any goalie in the NHL and was the only reason the Ducks were still in the hunt. But they flew south in the winter, losing 12 games in a row until Gibson stopped the bleeding with a shutout of the Minnesota Wild. After another win they went on a seven-game losing streak. That cost head coach Randy Carlyle his job and

Gibson his chance at any year-end silverware.

To add insult to injury, Gibson missed nine games with head and neck issues after teammate Jaycob Megna ran into him during a game in February, the latest in a string of unlucky injuries that began with a concussion and groin tear in his rookie season.

But adversity comes with the loneliest position in hockey, and Gibson is well acquainted with it.

Gibson, who started on defense but had so much fun blocking shots that he made it his job, played second-tier minor hockey and didn't even make the team at Baldwin High School in suburban Pittsburgh. But he used this setback as fuel for his rise.

Big and athletic, Gibson became a regular at area goalie schools and eventually caught the eye of the USA Hockey National Team Development Program. He went on to lead the U.S. to gold at the 2010 World Under-17 Challenge and 2011 Under-18 World Championship.

Later that year the Ducks chose Gibson with the 39th overall draft pick. He had committed to the University of Michigan but chose to join the Kitchener Rangers of the Ontario Hockey League instead, where he had matching .928 goals-against averages in his two seasons.

During his second year, Gibson had a World Juniors for the ages, leading Team USA to the gold medal in 2013 with the tournament's lowest goals-against average (1.36) and highest save percentage (.955). He was named a first-team all-star and won best goaltender and tournament MVP. He followed that up by posting a .951 save percentage at the 2013 World Championship to help the U.S. win bronze.

"We knew we had the best goalie in the world," said former USA Hockey National Team Development Program goalie coach Joe Exter after the World Juniors. "We saw the development take place over the

course of four years. We knew."

Gibson kept it up in the NHL. He shut out the Vancouver Canucks in his first game on April 7, 2014. He also blanked the eventual champion Los Angeles Kings in his first career postseason game in the second round of the 2014 playoffs after starter Frederik Andersen was injured. He was the youngest goalie in NHL history with a shutout in his playoff debut.

In 2015–16, Gibson shared the William M. Jennings Trophy with Andersen after playing 40 games and finishing with a 2.07 goals-against average, good for second in the NHL.

Prior to the 2016–17 season Andersen was traded to the Toronto Maple Leafs, making Gibson the undisputed number one. Gibson took the Ducks to the Western Conference Final, dispatching the Calgary Flames and Connor McDavid's Edmonton Oilers in the process before falling to the Nashville Predators.

Gibson had 60 starts in 2017–18 with a career-high .926 save percentage. The Ducks gave up the third-fewest goals against in the league and finished second in the Pacific Division with 101 points.

After the season Gibson got married, signed an eight-year contract worth an average of $6.4 million per season, and worked on core strength and flexibility so that he wouldn't fall victim to repetitive stress injuries. Even with the injury in February he played 58 games in 2018–19 and deservedly won nine of his last 11 starts to finish the season of turmoil.

Gibson's career .921 save percentage (minimum 100 games played) is tied for second in the NHL since his first full season. Solid goaltending is solid gold and the Ducks will stay in the game as long as they have their 6-foot-2, 206-pound star goalie backing them up.

"Since Gibson played in Kitchener he's been destined for greatness," said former NHL goalie and NHL Network analyst Kevin Weekes in early 2019. "Expected to be great — and he's delivered at every stage. Every level of competition. What you're seeing is exactly what he has been and is. Dominant."

Won gold and was named best goaltender at the 2011 Under-18 World Championship

Won gold and was named best goaltender and tournament MVP at the 2013 World Junior Championship

Named to the NHL All-Rookie Team in 2016

Played in the 2019 NHL All-Star Game

PLAYER INDEX

Aho, Sebastian	70	Faulk, Justin	76	Laine, Patrik	108	Scheifele, Mark	88
Andersen, Frederik	42	Fleury, Marc-André	132	Larkin, Dylan	36	Seguin, Tyler	96
				Lehner, Robin	80	Stamkos, Steven	22
Backstrom, Nicklas	58	Gaudreau, Johnny	122	Letang, Kris	54	Stone, Mark	150
Barkov, Aleksander	32	Gibson, John	156			Subban, P.K.	104
Barzal, Mathew	72	Giordano, Mark	130	MacKinnon, Nathan	86	Suter, Ryan	116
Bergeron, Patrice	8	Giroux, Claude	60	Malkin, Evgeni	62		
Bishop, Ben	106	Gostisbehere, Shayne	78	Marchand, Brad	20	Tarasenko, Vladimir	112
Bobrovsky, Sergei	56			Matthews, Auston	12	Tavares, John	24
Boeser, Brock	146	Hall, Taylor	48	McDavid, Connor	126	Theodore, Shea	154
Burns, Brent	128	Hedman, Victor	14	Monahan, Sean	148	Toews, Jonathan	98
Byfuglien, Dustin	114	Holtby, Braden	68				
				Ovechkin, Alex	50	Vasilevskiy, Andrei	30
Carlson, John	64	Jones, Martin	144				
Chabot, Thomas	38	Jones, Seth	52	Pavelski, Joe	136	Weber, Shea	16
Crosby, Sidney	46	Josi, Roman	90	Pettersson, Elias	138	Werenski, Zach	66
				Pietrangelo, Alex	102	Wheeler, Blake	100
Dahlin, Rasmus	40	Kane, Patrick	84	Price, Carey	18		
Doughty, Drew	140	Karlsson, Erik	142			Yandle, Keith	28
Draisaitl, Leon	134	Klingberg, John	92	Rantanen, Mikko	110		
Dubnyk, Devan	118	Kopitar, Anze	124	Rielly, Morgan	26	Zibanejad, Mika	74
		Kucherov, Nikita	10	Rinne, Pekka	94		
Eichel, Jack	34						
Ekman-Larsson, Oliver	152						

PHOTO CREDITS

Associated Press

Mark Humphrey: 92
Michael Dwyer: 4
Mike Wulf/CSM via ZUMA
    Wire: 28

Icon Sportswire

Adam Lacy: 52, 56
Andrew Bershaw: 31
Brett Holmes: 41, 83 (bottom),
    111, 119, 122, 131, 149,
    150
Cody Glenn: 136, 143
Curtis Comeau: 14, 24, 127,
    135
Daniel Bartel: 147
Danny Murphy: 90, 95, 97,
    104
David Berding: 83 (top), 118

David Kirouac: 6 (right), 17,
    18, 26, 45 (top), 54, 59, 76,
    121 (top), 130, 133, 148
Derek Cain: 23, 67, 71, 75,
    81, 82 (right), 87, 88, 96,
    109, 112, 123, 139, 146,
    155, 158
Douglas Stringer: 151
Fred Kfoury III: 8, 20, 66, 79,
    159
Gerry Angus: 91, 93
Greg Thompson: 61, 77
Jaylynn Nash: 36
Jeanine Leech: 6 (left), 9, 10,
    21, 33, 44 (left), 46, 47, 49,
    53, 55, 58, 62, 63, 68, 70,
    94, 98, 103, 105, 116, 120
    (right), 134, 142
Jeff Chevrier: 82 (left), 89

Jerome Davis: 34, 40
Joel Auerbach: 29, 32
John Cordes: 156
John Crouch: 45 (bottom), 80
John McCreary: 72
Joshua Lavallee: 125
Joshua Sarner: 44 (right), 60,
    74
Julian Avram: 25, 27
Keith Gillett: 100, 102, 107,
    108, 114, 126, 129, 153
Kyle Ross: 78
Mark Goldman: 69
Mark LoMoglio: 11, 138
Matt Cohen: 16, 121 (bottom),
    128, 137, 145, 154
Matthew Pearce: 106, 132, 144
Michael Tureski: 43, 157
Nick Turchiaro: 7 (top), 13, 42

Nick Wosika: 117
Patrick Gorski: 84, 85, 99, 152
Randy Litzinger: 64
Rich Graessle: 19, 35, 48, 73
Richard A. Whittaker: 30, 39,
    65, 120 (left) 124, 141
Rob Curtis: 140
Roy K. Miller: 15, 22
Russell Lansford: 86, 100
Scott W. Grau: 7 (bottom), 37
Steven King: 38
Terrence Lee: 101, 115
Tim Spyers: 113
Tony Quinn: 51
Vincent Ethier: 12, 50, 57

ACKNOWLEDGMENTS

Much love...

Julie, for her enormous patience and support.

Jag, Vik and Hollis, for the inspiration.

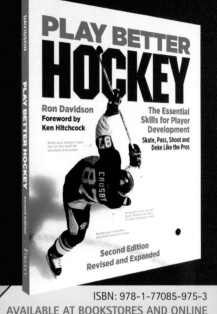
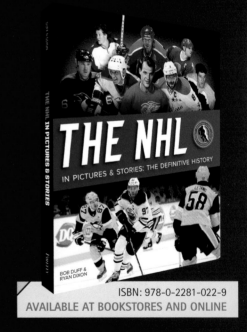